PT CRUISER

PERFORMANCE PROJECTS

D1227654

PT CRUISER

PERFORMANCE PROJECTS

ALAN PARADISE

MOTORBOOKS
INTERNATIONAL

Wholesalers & Distributors, Galtier Plaza, Suite 200, 380 Jackson Street, St. Paul, MN 55101-3885 USA.

About the author: Alan Paradise is credited with creating and developing Sport Compact Car magazine and served as its editor for the title's first four years. He also served on the staffs of numerous other niche-market publications, including Truckin', MiniTruckin', EuroSportCar, Street Rodder, Miata Magazine, Ragtops & Roadsters, British Motoring, Cruiser Quarterly, Celebrity Garage, Ford Racing's Inside The Oval, and SVT Enthusiast. He is also the founding editor of HCI magazine. Book credits include Civic Duty (2000) and Sport Compacts (2003). He also served as Guest Curator of "Tuner Revolution," an exhibit at the Petersen Automotive Museum in 2003. He is currently working as a writer and director on a series of automotive documentary films for Rhino Films. Paradise is a longtime performance enthusiast, owning and building a wide range of cars from classics to muscle cars, street rods, sports cars, and import performance cars.

ISBN 0-7603-1611-2

Editor: Peter Bodensteiner
Designer: LeAnn Kuhlmann
Printed in China

Contents

Dedication and Acknowledgments

In the world of automotive pop culture, some models become cult classics by accident. These would likely include the Mini Cooper, Datsun 510, Volkswagen Beetle, and Volvo PV544. These cars gained a following through a spontaneous explosion of enthusiasm. Then there are vehicles that, by their very design and market vibe, appeal to an enthusiast segment seemingly right off the drafting table. The PT Cruiser is such a vehicle. As part of Chrysler's retro-futurism trifecta (along with the Dodge Viper and Plymouth Prowler), the PT Cruiser helped bring the Chrysler crest back into the automotive spotlight.

This book celebrates not only the enormous popularity of the PT's original design, but also the ways it can be personalized to accentuate the passion of its owners.

During the creation of *PT Cruiser Performance Projects,* a number of people set aside time, effort, and materials to help in its production. Rob Taylor nearly let me disassemble and reassemble his flamed Cruiser on a number of occasions. Ray and Guy at PTeaser closed down their shop in Westminster for a few days to perform several of the tricks covered in the following pages.

It takes real confidence in your product to let a journalist follow the install of a pre-production item. That was the case when photographing the install of the Jackson Racing supercharger kit. Props to Mike Chapit and especially Oscar Jackson for allowing my camera to capture the first Jackson Racing supercharged PT.

As always, my biggest thanks go to my family. In the process of raising an 8-year year-old aspiring gearhead and Dogtown skater, as well as a 22-year-old off-road truck builder, I have all the inspiration I need to stay on the leading edge of youth-market pop culture. I often forget my age. Doing something you love will do that to you.

This book is also for my wife, Annette. Just when I think the gasoline and exhaust fumes circulating in the garage and permeating the entire household ventilation system are too much for a wife and mother to handle, when the tools are scattered across the floor and parts are stacked in every available shelf space, she never seems to feel like enough is enough. She keeps on listening to me and the boys ramble on about ignition timing, gear ratios, and suspension geometry. She never complains about the occasional grease spot on the carpet or oily clothes in the laundry. Through it all she finds a level of comfort, and even suggests subjects for future books and projects. Finding a partner who not only tolerates what you love to do, but also participates and encourages it, is truly a one-in-a-million find.

Introduction

Imagine you are an automotive designer with the ability to travel back in time. You transport yourself to the early 1920s and discover the formula for building inexpensive cars that can handle both people and cargo. You then set your time machine for the mid-1930s and marvel at the stylish sedans of the day. The 1960s progress with the birth of mass-produced front-wheel-drive cars. You wisely skip over the automotive wasteland of the 1970s and discover that the 1980s are disposable. Arriving back in the present day, you design a vehicle that would take the best of the past, then combine it with the technology of the present and the promise of the future.

Once you have the vehicle sketched out, you need to find a car company that is progressive and has the vision to understand the concept; it also must have the courage to undertake the project. That search lands you in Sterling Heights, Michigan, at the doorstep of Chrysler. Your design is a contemporary, personal transportation vehicle with all the technology of today and the style and charm of a bygone motoring era. The brain trust at Chrysler takes your lead and calls this new vehicle the PT Cruiser.

Okay, back to reality. It is highly unlikely anyone at Chrysler had stumbled across a flux capacitor or that Steven Spielberg had anything to do with the inspiration for the PT Cruiser. However, the brainwaves used to design, engineer, and build the most successful and innovative vehicle of our time certainly seem to come from a company that was looking to the past for its inspiration.

By looking to the past, Chrysler pushed the styling of the future with the PT Cruiser. The company created "retro-futurism" and forever changed the entrenched patterns of the automotive industry. The PT Cruiser project was destined for success even before the first production car rolled off the assembly line. By bringing back the distinction of fenders to the hood and semi-running boards while pulling away from the egg-shaped "can't tell if it/s coming or going" styling that has permeated the auto industry, the entire idea of the PT has captured the imagination of consumers.

The automotive world has been hard pressed to define what a PT Cruiser is—car, truck, SUV, or station wagon. No matter what category or tag is put on the PT, it is always accompanied by the one term that best describes the vehicle, "cool."

Chrysler first intended the PT for a young, entry-level demographic. Instead, PT buyers are well beyond the original target-market age of 18-to 32-year-old buyers. However, the entry-level data was right on target—just not in the way Chrysler had in mind.

PT owners turned out to be entry level in the world of performance and personalizing. This is the impetus for this book.

In this book, you will discover a number of projects designed to enhance the joy and personal pride you have for your PT Cruiser. Each project or modification is broken down by what is needed to complete the job. And while this is not a step-by-step installation

manual, it will give you a good idea of what is involved, as well as the time and skill it will require to achieve desirable results.

Included are tips about the social aspect of being a PT Cruiser enthusiast. This is a very important and prominent part of ownership. Not since the introduction of the Mazda Miata has a vehicle captured the hearts of so many. The major difference is that Chrysler's production numbers are three times greater than the number of Miatas built and sold by Mazda over the same introduction period.

One reason the PT Cruiser is so popular is its styling, which inspires us to add personal touches and make each a one-of-a-kind creation—an extension of our image and imagination.

With that in mind, it's time to dig in and improve your Cruiser.

Before You Begin

Tools

Nothing can make working on a vehicle more pleasurable than having the right tools. In sharp contrast, not having the right tools can add tremendous frustration to any project. Therefore, acquiring and maintaining a quality set of tools is vital. Owning the right tools is a real confidence builder. A good set of tools also saves time (making installation quicker) and money (reducing the risk of damaging nuts, bolts, and screws).

Tools are available in varying levels of quality. The low-end tools can be poor quality, easily broken, and awkward to use. The grip, fit, and finish are often substandard. Despite the allure of a low price, it is best to invest more money to get far more usable work mates.

Brands such as Craftsman, Husky, or Mastercraft are more mid-level. Each of these companies provides a lifetime warranty because each item meets very good standards. Most of the time these are the ideal tools for weekend mechanics. With a little diligent shopping, you can purchase a basic package for a reasonable price.

Professional-grade tools from companies such as Snap-On or Mac are state-of-the-art. They are durable, precise, and comfortable to use. Yet, these tools do require a serious outlay of money. If you can afford them, you will not be disappointed. However, it may be better to spend the money on your PT, rather than on professional-grade tools.

What's in Your Toolbox?

Working on your PT Cruiser is quite easy. Chrysler found ways to simplify nearly every conceivable procedure. In many cases, one tool can do an entire job. While not completely necessary (as most of the work will require metric wrenches and sockets) it is recommended that you stock your toolbox with both metric and standard tools.

Socket Sets

A good socket set is the first place for you to start. A set of 3/8-inch drive sockets that range from 10 millimeters to 24 millimeters will cover just about any job in this book. Get both shallow and deep sockets. A handle extension (breaker bar) is very useful when it comes to loosening components that

Good, quality tools don't have to be expensive. Shop around and look for sales. Many sets will offer most of the necessary items for a lower price. This is especially true for socket sets.

the factory attached with air wrenches. Socket extensions will be useful as well. At the outset, this may seem like a large laundry list of tools. However, it is quite common to find tool sets that have 95 percent of what you will need.

Wrenches

Along with sockets, standard combination wrenches are invaluable. These have an open end and a closed end. The size range is the same as with sockets. The thinner heads of quality tools will make it easier to reach hidden fasteners. Whenever possible, use the closed end of the wrench to avoid damage to bolt heads.

Screwdrivers

Screw heads are the easiest fasteners to strip. We have all done it before, and in the process, we have also selected a number of choice phrases to describe our affection for the maker of the screws. To avoid this

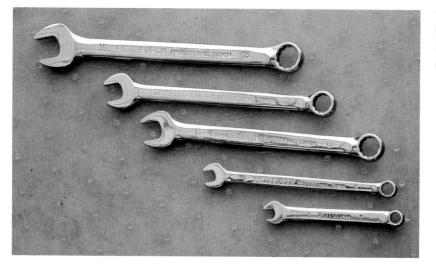

You can also find wrench sets for a reasonable price. It is advisable to purchase both metric and standard sizes.

level of agony, stock your toolbox with a minimum of three sizes of Phillips (cross) screwdrivers and flat-head drivers. Magnetized drivers can be a plus when they are required to remove and/or secure screws in hard-to-reach areas. In addition, retractable grippers, a magnetic rod, or driver blade are very useful when you drop a screw or bolt (and you will) into areas that are impossible to reach by hand.

Torque Wrench
Although it is an expensive piece of equipment, intelligent use of a torque wrench can make the difference between a professional-level job and being branded a shade tree mechanic. The most common is the click-type that can be set to the appropriate torque and then clicks when that value is reached. The beam-style is inexpensive and works, but it can be difficult to read in tight spaces. Electronic torque wrenches work well for engine builders and professional mechanics, but they are overkill for a home garage.

Jacks and Jack Stands
A good hydraulic jack is very useful, along with four jack stands. A jack and stands rated for two tons should do the job. Heavier jacks are sometimes

Universal joint sockets and ratchet extensions can be valuable assets.

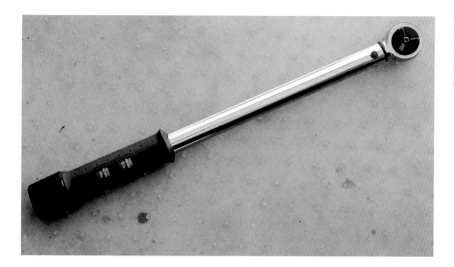

Take the guesswork out of securing vital fasteners by using a torque wrench. No toolbox should be lacking this instrument.

difficult to fit underneath the car. Think about your safety while under your PT Cruiser. Saving $10 or $20 on jack stands won't seem that important when you are looking at the underside of the vehicle from your creeper. Speaking of creepers, they're cool, useful, and make working on your back bearable. The downside to a creeper is trying to keep your kids from using it like a Flexi-Flyer.

Pry Bars and Hammers

When you need to get physical, nothing says testosterone like a good pry bar. A pry bar will come into play when you are working on the suspension, and at times under the hood. As for a hammer, it's all about gentle persuasion. For the most part, all you need is a simple tap from your hammer.

Pliers

Needle-nose pliers can be a good substitute for fingers, especially in tight places. Bullnose pliers can be used for grabbing, twisting, and holding. Vice-grips (or molegrips) are ideal for applying more force but can be hard on parts; use them with some level of restraint.

Options

There are a number of other useful tools. The key is to determine the need-to-have from the nice-to-have. Air tools, spring compressors, hoists, punches, and safety wire pliers can be used at the right time. Most are one-time-use tools, and it is best to borrow them from a friend or rent them for a day.

Workplace and Surface

Your work environment is critical to the success of the project. Whenever possible, a garage is the ideal place to take on any project that requires more than two hours to complete. This is because working outdoors, exposed to heat, moisture, wind, and airborne contaminants, can quickly beat down even the hardiest of workers. A garage protects you and your PT from the elements, and you will have space to organize everything in a secure enclosure. Most garages also offer a concrete floor, which is a preferable surface for working on or under your PT. If you must suspend your PT on a jack, jack stands, or ramps, a level concrete surface is your best bet for safety. Never work under your PT when the vehicle is on dirt, grass, or gravel. An asphalt surface, while more solid than dirt or grass, can become soft and somewhat unstable as it heats up. This could lead to the jacks and stands sinking into the surface, and it could disrupt the stability of the vehicle.

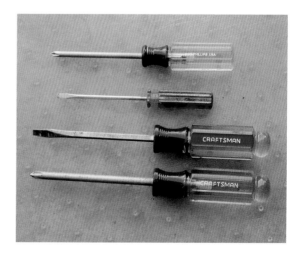

During the course of personalizing your PT, both Phillips and standard screwdrivers will be necessary.

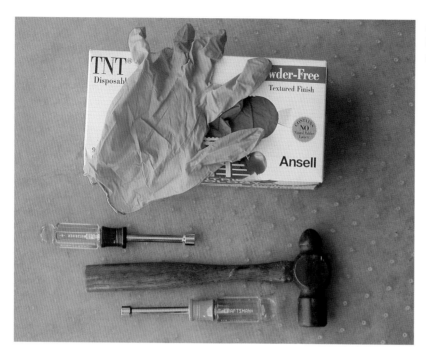

A few other handy items include a hammer, nut drivers, and latex gloves.

No Substitute for Safety

The urge to complete a project can become so powerful that you will be tempted to compromise safety in favor of reducing installation time. Let me put this simply—don't do it. Safety concerns should always be your first priority. It doesn't matter how much better your PT will look or perform if you are not around to enjoy it.

Other items will assist you when working on any vehicle. Latex gloves can help protect your hands from grease and many abrasive automotive chemicals. Gloves also can improve grip and ease cleanup. Safety glasses or goggles are important to help keep debris and chemicals from causing eye damage. It is always better to prepare for safety and err on the side of caution.

Summing Up

Before you set out to improve the Cruiser, here is one last word of advice: Be as cool as your car. Not all projects go as smoothly as the instructions indicate. There are going to be glitches and speed bumps along the way. Take it slow and easy. Check, double check, and triple check all fits and measurements before your final installation. Above all, remember that you are altering a vehicle beyond the manufacturer's engineering and dealing with aftermarket components. Select each wisely with quality fit and finish in mind. Since the PT Cruiser community is quite social, it is likely that other PT owners have performed a similar modification and can offer you some additional words of wisdom. Once you have completed each modification, you will have gained the knowledge and wisdom to help other PT owners. You may even want to suggest this book to a friend.

You may not want to throw down cash for a spring compressor. However, reasonably priced items do exist. Perhaps this is something your local PT Cruiser club may want to purchase for the use of its members.

PROJECT 1 ★ *Building on a Budget*

There it is—your new Chrysler PT Cruiser. Your mind begins to run wild with ideas of how you can create your personal transportation statement and, in the process, find ways to fall deeper in love with your new road mate. Even the factory PT Cruisers are above-average-looking vehicles. Even the most humble models are capable of turning heads. As cool as these vehicles are, however, there is so much that can be done. The hood houses stock air box, intake manifold, engine cover, and other various factory components. The suspension features about 5 inches of wheel well gap on the rear and gives the vehicle a 1970s "stink bug" appearance. Some owners find the performance a bit on the sluggish side, while others desire to improve the overall handling and drivability of their PT.

You envision custom paint, 18-inch wheels, lowered suspension, tuned exhaust, leather interior, a crisp, clean audio system, and traveling 0 to 60 miles per hour in less than the current 10 seconds. How do you get there?

It is safe to assume that, for most of us, our PT use is primarily for daily transportation. Since this is the case, it is important that the vehicle has the ability to perform daily functions with relative ease and without the fear of canceling the factory warranty or your insurance company's roadside assistance program. This makes it important to plan the modifications and remain within a useful scope of practicality. From this point, we can explore the different avenues for contemporary PT Cruiser modifications and personalization.

If you are dreaming of a pure show vehicle, you need to be aware of the pros and cons of building one. Sure, everyone will be looking with envy at your PT and it will fill more than a few fireplace mantels with trophies, but there is a cost. The first major change is that you will be less likely to drive the vehicle due to fear of damage. The second problem is that building a show-stopper requires a major investment.

A street-custom approach (by far the most popular option) gives you a PT designed to add some level of show, a bit more go, and all the usefulness needed to drive in relative comfort and with reliability.

Although not yet a major factor, building a PT for racing can be a rewarding challenge. Recent technological advancements have created performance options that can provide your PT with greater acceleration, improved handling, and precise braking.

There are many ways to outfit your PT Cruiser, but there are only two ways to achieve the final result. The two methods are called *addition* and *subtraction*. Either method will take time and cost you money. However, one is far more efficient and cost effective.

Addition, the practice of adding parts and features as you go, is the most common method used to construct any personalized vehicle. Addition often results in purchasing many parts that are later discarded. Unplanned actions serve only as a quick fix for a modification habit that is not kept in check by logic. A common term used for this type of customizing is called "impulse buying."

Subtraction is planning how you want your PT to end up and working in reverse to achieve the desired goal. This might seem backward, but is a very sound method for realizing the final achievement.

Working in subtraction requires you to develop a personalized build sheet. Start by visualizing the finished PT in contrast to the PT you actually have. Now begin to assemble, on paper, the components it will take to get to your dream version.

Let's start with a factory-stock version, and build a street version using both addition and subtraction methods.

Concept and reality. The Buckaroo PT started life as a rendering in black, but it became a reality in red. This was one of the first PT Cruisers to make its way to the public, thus color availability was limited.

ADDITION

Step One : You want a lower, performance-looking stance. You purchase and install 3-inch lowering springs.

Step Two : The factory 16-inch tires and wheels look "tucked" into the fender wells, which is good, but no amount of lowering will change the fact these are stock tires and wheels. You purchase 17x7-inch wheels and 235/40-17 tires.

Step Three : Performance becomes an issue because now your PT is slower than when it was stock. Reason? The larger tread surface of the tires and the increased weight of the wheels cause the greater drag. You buy into the performance exhaust theory, hoping to regain the lost engine response. You buy a 3-inch exhaust system and throw on a chrome tip. Is the problem solved?

Plan out your PT's look in advance. This slick street/salt-flat racer version would be a fairly simple and realistic conversion. All the aftermarket components exist and are easy to install.

Step Four : Still hungry for horsepower, you need an air intake system, but you're a little short on funds after spending $600 on the exhaust system. Price influences your buying decision, and within a few days, a short pipe system arrives at your doorstep. You install the trendy painted piece and prepare for neck-snapping acceleration gains. Reality checks in when the 3 to 5 horsepower gain is hardly noticeable.

Step Five : With major funds depleted, you feed your habit by doing smaller, less expensive additions: Line wrap, small polished or chrome-plated trinkets, pedal covers, etc.

Step Six : You discover the ride quality of the suspension combination is too harsh. The problem is the lubricant leaking from your shocks. They have blown out because the spring rate was not compatible with the shock rebound. You purchase performance shocks.

Step Seven : You smarten up and start doing modifications in "Subtraction."

BUILDING IN SUBTRACTION

Step One : You use your PT for a few weeks as a general means of transportation. This seems like torture, but these few weeks will help you understand your Chrysler product and you will learn how the vehicle is engineered. It also gives you a better feel for the horsepower and handling gains you'll realize later.

Step Two : Create a special "Build Sheet" for your car. This will start out as a wish list. Over time, it will become a blueprint. You may find it helpful to know what your local and state laws are regarding emissions control devices, body modifications, lighting, exhaust noise, etc. This research will head off a potential problem later.

Step Three : Determine your PT's most critical area of need. If it is horsepower gains you desire, this is the time to perform extensive engine modifications. If only minor engine modifications and dress-up are likely, you will want to consider the body and paint work first. If the ride height is too unbearable to deal with, start with the tires, wheels, and springs.

Step Four : Learn discipline. Remember, unless you're a lotto winner, you can't do everything at once . . . and you really don't want to do that anyway. It's more fun to stretch out the process. This allows you to get to know the tricks and trends along the way.

Step Five : Research the equipment in each area. Engine, exterior, suspension, interior, transmission, audio, paint, and body. The more you know about

Turning a PT into a Carson top version requires only that you follow many of the modifications in this book and see your local trim shop for the 1950s padded-top material.

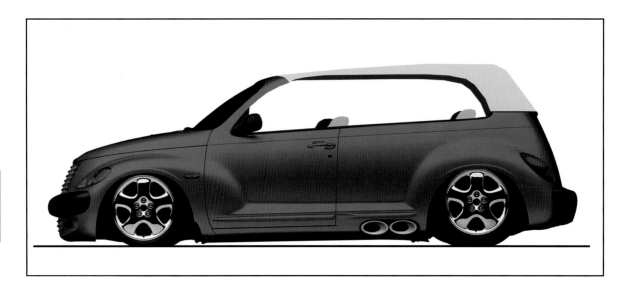

With the release of the convertible, the Phaeton top conversion is possible.

the history and reliability of the products you want, the better shopper you will be.

Step Six: Prioritize your building . . . and begin.

At right are the most common "bolt-on" after-market products for PT Cruisers and how they fit into each of the basic build groups.

Using mail-order ads, Internet sites, and local retailers, attach a price to each of the items you have on your build sheet. With all the cost factors in hand, you can make intelligent decisions about how to achieve your goal. If you have unlimited funds, you could build by category: engine, suspension, interior, exterior, etc. For the vast majority of us, it will be necessary to budget the build-up. A custom build sheet will offer you a unique reference point for conducting your work.

PRODUCT	STREET	STRIP	SHOW	LOWRIDER	RETRO
ENGINE					
COLD AIR INDUCTOION					
CHROME COVERS					
PERFORMANCE IGNITION					
FORCED INDUCTION					
PERFORMANCE EXHAUST					
SUSPENSION					
PERFORMANCE SPRINGS					
LOWERING SPRINGS					
PERFORMANCE SHOCKS					
ANTI-ROLL BARS					
UPPER STRUT TIE BAR					
17-INCH WHEELS					
18-INCH WHEELS					
20-INCH WHEELS					
PERFORMANCE TIRES					
URETHANE BUSHINGS					
HYDRAULICS					
PERFORMANCE BRAKES					
AIR RIDE ASSIST					
TRANSMISSION					
PERFORMANCE CLUTCH					
SHORT THROW SHIFTER					
EXTERIOR STYLING					
FRONT AIR DAM					
FENDER SKIRTS					
REAR VALANCE/ROLL PAN					
REAR SPOILER					
RAM AIR HOOD					
DRIVING LIGHTS					
TAILLIGHT COVERS					
TINTED WINDOWS					
CUSTOM PAINT					
INTERIOR STYLING					
LEATHER SEATING					
RACING SEATS					
HARNESS BELTS					
GAUGES					
SUNROOF					
PEDAL COVERS					
SILL PLATES					
CUSTOM SHIFT KNOB					

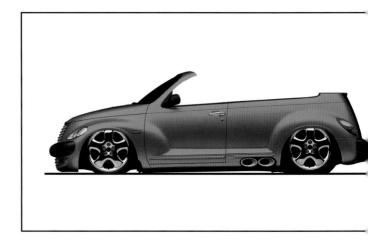

Of course, a dropped and tricked-out roadster is a sweet ride with the right stance and exterior modifications.

PROJECT 2 ★ *Getting Your PT Road-Ready*

Time: **3 hours**

Tools: **Shop rag, air pressure gauge, oil spout, transmission funnel, plastic container**

Talent: ★

Tab: **$150**

Parts: **Flares, first aid kit, flat fixer, maps, spare belts, oil, brake fluid, coolant**

Tip: **Make a list, then check it twice**

Benefit: **It is better to have something and not need it than to need something and not have it**

Before you embark on a road trip to any number of PT Cruiser events, it is wise to perform an overall safety inspection of your PT. Even if it just has a few thousand miles on the odometer, you should make sure everything is in good working order and that you bring items you may need. Having the right items in a time of need can make the difference between a good experience and the road trip from hell. If you plan to caravan to the event with a group or your local club, get together to do a mass vehicle inspection. This would be a fun club activity and those that are more knowledgeable can help those that are still learning about automotive maintenance.

Start by looking over the suspension components. Make sure that your tires have enough tread on them and look for nails or other items that may lead to a punctured tire or slow air leak. A simple test for checking tread depth involves placing a penny between the tread blocks. Rotate the penny so that Lincoln's head is upside down. The tread should be deep enough to reach the top of Lincoln's head. If the tread is worn, you may have problems with hydroplaning if you're caught in a rainstorm. Also check the tire pressure of all four tires and the spare tire. A flat spare tire won't be very useful. Loose lug nuts are bad news, so check to see that they are all properly tightened (100 ft-lbs of torque).

Take a look under the car and check for loose nuts and bolts on all suspension parts. Visually inspect the shocks to make sure they are not leaking fluid. Inspect the brake rotors and pads. There should be a good amount of pad material left—look for the pad material to be at least as wide as the pad's backing plate. The rotors should be smooth and free of any unusual grooves or cracks.

Turn on your headlights and hazard flashers. Walk around your PT to ensure everything is working properly. Hop inside the vehicle and check the horn, windows, air conditioning, windshield wipers, heater, and, of course, the audio system. If your neighbors come over to complain, then you know that the audio system is working properly.

Before you climb out, pull the hood release lever and poke your head into the engine bay. Check all fluid levels including brake, oil, transmission, power

Bring extra fluids and lubricants such as motor oil, brake fluid, and spray lube. An oil spout will also come in handy.

Having a few important items such as a jack, tire pressure gauge, basic tools, a shop towel, gloves, and duct tape could mean the difference between making a simple repair and taking a long walk to the next town.

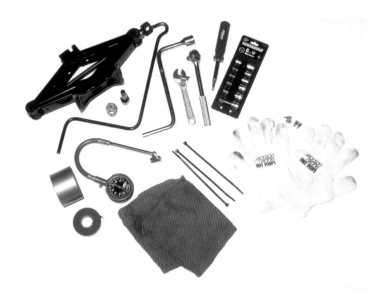

steering, windshield washer fluid, and coolant. If it has been a while since the last oil change, now is a good time to do that as well. Inspect hoses and belts for signs of wear and cracks. Also look at the engine wiring to see if anything is loose or worn. Check the operation of the throttle return spring by rotating the mechanism until the throttle is wide open, then releasing it. It should return to the fully closed position without sticking and provide plenty of resistance when you rotate it open. If your battery has been giving you problems lately, replacing it before the trip is a good idea.

After completing a basic safety inspection, make a checklist of items to bring with you. Start with the safety items such as a fire extinguisher, a First Aid kit, a mobile phone, a flashlight, flares, and drinking water. A note pad and pen will come in handy for writing down insurance and contact information if an accident occurs, or for directions. It's also a good idea to hide some extra cash somewhere in your car in case you lose your wallet or need some extra cash for food and supplies.

In the event that something does go wrong with your car, pack some supplies for basic repairs. Put together a small toolkit including various sockets, wrenches, screwdrivers, and the ever-useful duct tape. Verify that the spare tire, jack, and lug wrench are in the proper location. If you have locking lugs, don't forget to bring the key. A can of tire sealant can often be a lifesaver. Bring an extra accessory belt and some extra spark plugs. Spare fuses and electrical tape can help to solve minor electrical problems along the way. Grab some various extra fluids such as two quarts of motor oil, some coolant, WD-40, and brake fluid. A set of gloves and some rags will help keep you clean should you need to perform minor repairs on the road.

In the passenger glove compartment, have the event address and phone numbers with you. Take a map of the course as well as a camera and film. But most of all, don't forget to bring music with you.

Unless you're a big fan of country music, CDs or tapes are a must since the radio station selection in some areas can be limited.

You may be asking yourself, "How much space is all this stuff going to take?" For the most part, all the aforementioned items can fit in a small cardboard box or a gym-size duffel bag. In a PT Cruiser, this leaves plenty of space for clothes, cleaning supplies, and any trophies you'll be coming home with. Keep in mind that getting there can be half the fun.

Be sure to bring a map to verify your destination as well as a security device if you have to leave your vehicle unattended. A hat, sunscreen, and sunglasses are a must.

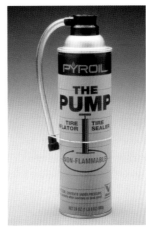

Above: Check the air pressure on all tires, including the spare.

Above right: Safety equipment such as flares, a fire extinguisher, a flashlight, and a First Aid kit are very important.

Right: Tire sealant ranks among one of the best automotive inventions to date. It can be a real lifesaver if you somehow have the misfortune of getting two flats.

ROAD TRIP CHECKLIST
Items to Check

Suspension
Tire condition and tread
Tire pressure
Wheel alignment
Lug nuts
Shock absorber function and condition
Condition of brake rotors

Safety Equipment
Headlights
Taillights
Brake lights
Turn signals
Horn
Door locks

Interior
Window operations
Air conditioning
Heater
Windshield defroster
Audio system

Under the Hood
Oil level (change oil if necessary)
Coolant level
Windshield washer fluid level
Engine clean
Accessory (fan) belt condition
Battery condition
Battery cables

Condition of ignition wires
Spark plug gaps and condition
Brake fluid
Throttle return spring
Radiator hoses (feed and return)

Stuff to bring
Spare tire (check tire pressure)
Tire inflation product
Mobile phone
Spare accessory/fan belt
Abbreviated tool kit
Extra coolant
WD-40
Two quarts of oil

PROJECT 3 ★ *Joining the PT Cruiser Community*

Time: The entire ownership experience

Tools: Good will, cooperation

Talent: ★

Tab: Priceless

Parts: A brain and good heart

Tip: Get involved

Benefit: Completes the thrill of ownership

If you're in an area where there are more than five other PT Cruisers, there is a high probability that some sort of enthusiasts' club exists. A club provides you with an opportunity to seek out other PT Cruiser owners and to intensify your personal ownership bliss.

Getting involved in a local club can provide an ideal blend of camaraderie and education. For PT owners, this is usually a social setting that helps move the ownership experience forward and enables us to become more attached to the vehicle and its special qualities. It is a vital and specific ingredient in the overall pleasure of owning a car that has quickly become one of the most popular enthusiasts' vehicles in automotive history. To date, only the Model T Ford, Volkswagen Beetle, Mazda Miata, Ford Mustang, and Chevrolet Corvette have ownership groups that rival the size and enthusiasm of the PT Cruiser community.

On a national level, there are several associations (PT Cruiser Club, MobilRelay Affinity Group, PTOC) where PT Cruiser owners can find benefit in membership. A few of these national ownership organizations have regional divisions and local chapters. By attending local chapter meetings and through participation in various events, your passion for your retro-futurist machine can be greatly accelerated.

In the days when the cars that inspired the PT Cruiser were the fuel for enthusiasts' passion (before the Internet), locating a local club was usually a hit-or-miss situation. This is because most local clubs were not well organized or tightly run. Therefore, you needed to be in the right place at the right time in order to be approached by a member of an existing club. Today the Internet has made it far easier to locate national and local clubs. A few clicks of the mouse can get you the contact information for many owners' groups in any given geographical area . . . even rural Iowa and Nebraska.

While in the process of selecting a local club, attend two or three meetings before becoming a full-fledged member. Even participate in an event or two as a nonmember. This will give you an opportunity

Clubs help form a community of owners—people who enjoy the same interest in the PT Cruiser as you do.

Clubs can grow quickly. Therefore, being organized and forward-thinking is vital to maintaining order and proper structure.

to observe club members in action. In some cases, the inner politics of clubs can detract from the fun of just getting together to further the enjoyment of ownership. For others, a more rigid club structure brings greater group comfort.

Most well-formed and well-run clubs will operate with a code of conduct set forth in the bylaws. Once you're comfortable with the club, it's time to become a member and perhaps even adorn your PT with the club's logo.

One thing's for sure—when you're in a club there is not a shortage of opinions.

From showroom stock to radical custom, a good club accepts them all. The quality of the owner is more important than the quantity of the vehicle's modifications.

There is the possibility that a local club does not exist or none of the established clubs have met with your and your family's standards, needs, or desires. Starting your own club may be the best option.

Before getting your club together, attend local street rod and musclecar club meetings. Many of these clubs have survived for decades by inventing and reinventing themselves to meet with their members' changing wants and needs. In addition, classic, street rod, and musclecar clubs have social and economic demographics that are similar to those of the PT owners you will be encountering during your membership drives. Going to other car club meetings will expose you to items and procedures you may want to incorporate into your club. The key is to absorb everything and extract the better elements and discard (but don't forget) the useless parts.

Getting the word out on the street will require being smart and organized. First, design easy-to-read club flyers to attract potential members. Go to as many events and cruise nights as possible. The more your club's name and logo get out there, the more known the club will become.

The first order of business is to establish a strong set of club bylaws. Be forewarned that this will prevent some PT Cruiser owners from becoming involved. It will, however, bring your club respect and ultimately attract the best PT enthusiasts. Next, you will need a good, centrally located meeting place. Be careful to select a place with plenty of parking. In many cases, your local Chrysler dealership can be an ideal location because meetings are usually held at night and dealer meeting rooms are unoccupied. This arrangement can be attractive to the dealership as well because it keeps Chrysler owners coming through the door, and it increases the probability of future sales and service.

The most important factor in running a club is inclusion. It is a mistake to judge potential members by the quality of the PT Cruisers they drive. Tricked out or bone stock, the vehicle is less important than the member it carries. It is more important to have quality members than show-

You never know where a club membership is going to take you. At far left is Al Jardine (one of the original members of the Beach Boys), having some fun with members of the PT Owners Club, including President Manley Bland (second from left).

winning Cruisers. Set up the meetings and events to include the input of all the members . . . not just the officers.

The growth of the club will come with involvement in events outside PT Cruiser circles. To accomplish this, encourage participation in events promoted by other local car clubs. This demonstrates your club's willingness to become an active part of the entire car club community.

The club you decide to join or run will be your fingerprint on the car club world. Choose wisely, act responsibly, and above all, have fun.

PROJECT 4 ★ Selecting Tires and Wheels

Time: **As long as it takes**

Tools: **Telephone, phone book, computer, Internet access**

Talent: ★

Tab: **$1,000 – $4,000**

Parts: **Tires, wheels, lug nuts**

Tip: **Research the market; consider wheel weight, tire tread pattern and compound. Insist that balancing weights be mounted on the inside of the wheel rim. Clock the tires and wheels for show PTs.**

Benefit: **Better road manners, improved handling, competition appearance**

Most experienced performance car builders agree that a successful construction begins with the tires, wheels, and springs. The upcoming projects will cover picking the correct suspension components. Let's move to selecting the tire and wheel combination that best fits your needs and wants.

Large-diameter 18- to 20-inch wheels provide an impressive appearance, but the rubber-band sidewalls of 35- and 40-aspect tires make for a rough ride. That's right, the tires play as big a role in determining ride quality as the springs.

Knowing the language of tires will give you a better idea of the different levels and qualities associated with performance tires. Take a 235/45-17 tire. What do the numbers mean?

235= The width of the tire in millimeters, measured from sidewall to sidewall.

45= This number is the aspect ratio of the tire. It describes the height of the sidewall in relation to the width of the tire. The lower the number, the shorter the sidewall.

17= The diameter of the inside of the tire, in inches. This tire would require a 17-inch wheel.

If you're building your PT Cruiser as a daily driver, the most common tire and wheel combination needed is a 17x7 or 17x7.5-inch wheels on 235/40-17 tires. It is possible to extend the choices to 18-, 19-, and even 20-inch tire and wheel sizes. It has been proven, however, that 17- and 18-inch combinations generally provide an excellent appearance and allow for reasonable road compliance.

Before purchasing any wheel, pick it up and compare the weight of one wheel to another. The heavier the wheel, the more energy it will require to move it. Multiply the added weight by four and you can better understand the potential for significant power losses due to bigger wheels. Aluminum is lighter than steel, component wheels are lighter than cast wheels, and magnesium wheels are lighter than air. (Magnesium wheels were first used in racing because of their extremely light weight. The style became popular, thus the term "mag wheel" was born. Although these wheels are light, they do not fare well when subjected to everyday street use.)

Selecting a wheel and tire fitment can be a complicated and confusing decision process. A properly selected wheel/tire combo is worth the investment.

Above & left: Here are two similarly painted PTs with distinctively different appearances. The 5-spoke, 18-inch combo is tucked for the street rod look. The European multi-spoke wheels add a touch of street elegance to the vehicle.

Below: Selecting the right tires and wheels is the key to visually transforming your PT from mild to wild. Too big, and the tires will stick out of the fenders (not good). Too small, and the vehicle will look under-tired (also not good). Getting it right is important.

First, explore the intended use and driving style for your PT. Many driving conditions allow for low-profile tires year-round. Other road-going circumstances, such as cold or rainy climates, may require more forethought. Next, consider the basic details of your PT's suspension. Are you intending to utilize Chrysler's original underpinnings or will the vehicle have a combination of factory and aftermarket components?

For the most part, the wheel companies do a reasonably good job at developing proper fitments. Many full-service wheel and tire retail operations have the combinations already planned out.

Not too long ago, 18-inch wheels were the cutting edge. However, 19- and 20-inch wheels are

Here, billet aluminum wheels add to the retro-rod theme.

now being used with the right tire selections, even on lowered vehicles. The "Plus" sizing for wheel and tire combinations—which essentially means that as the wheel grows in diameter, the sidewall height becomes smaller—keeps the overall circumference the same as factory (or very close). Not only does this help with fitment, but it also makes speedometer recalibration unnecessary. Tires sized 235/35 will work on 18-inch wheels in the front, and thanks to slightly wider rear wheel wells, the rears can be 245/35-18.

The bulk of wheel manufacturers are happy to inform enthusiasts of their available styles. Tire and wheel outlets and custom PT builders display numerous innovative wheel and tire combinations. Many can combine these selections with popular suspension components to achieve the most desirable appearance.

Speaking of retro-rod, how about giant whites and chrome smoothies? This is a very popular look on many PTs.

A good rule of thumb in the customizing world is that the gap between the top of the tire and the apex of the fender should be no greater than the sidewall of the tire.

Wheel and tire sizes that work on PT Cruisers run from 15x7 on 205/50-15 tires to 20-inch wheels with 30-profile tires. Tire width ranges from 205 to 235 millimeters in front and up to 245 millimeters in back.

Another crucial measurement is wheel offset. The offset determines how the wheel and tire are centered in the wheel well, as well as how far the wheel and tire are from the inner well and fender lip. The magic offset for the PT Cruiser appears to be 35 millimeters, but there is a give-or-take of up to 10 millimeters.

Many suspension spring options exist for the PT. Before making a decision, consider how you plan to drive. You could do a drastic drop or lower your car barely more than an inch front and rear. Big drops make wheel and tire fitment more critical, because the package will have to be more exact. Adjustable coil-over and air bag kits are also on the market, providing infinite adjustability and maximum drop. All of this will affect your wheel and tire fitment. Too much drop can cause you to bottom out the suspension or cause the tire to contact the wheel well or fender lip. This can happen on bumps, during acceleration or braking, during lateral movement (cornering load), or when you're carrying a heavy load in your PT.

Also consider the shape of the tire. Factory 195/65-15 tires have a much rounder sidewall-to-tread edge than a 235/40-18, although the overall circumference is nearly identical. This will affect how the tire fits into the wheel well, making precise backspacing critical. Backspacing is the location of the wheels' mounting holes and their relation to the rim depth. This location will determine how close the tire and wheel will be to the edge of the fender well and suspension components.

The purpose you have planned for your PT could rule out a large number of choices, making the selection process much simpler. If you're going retro-rod, 17-inch or larger wheels might not look right or period-correct. You may want to use a wide 15- or 16-inch tire with a lot of sidewall to it, perhaps with whitewalls or raised white letters. If you're riding the tuner-car trend, 17-inch-or-larger wheel-and-tire packages will be the better choice. If your PT is destined for showing and cruising, options that are even more aggressive may be the right course. Price becomes a bigger issue as you go up the scale, though, as the 16-inch wheels and tires are often half the price of 19s.

Wheel and tire fitment is a balancing act and a poorly chosen wheel and tire combination can ruin your driving experience. However, if a great deal of planning and thought are involved in your choice, your PT Cruiser's wheels and tires will look good and provide a large dose of satisfaction.

SPEED RATING YOUR TIRE SELECTION

The letter included in the tire size specifications imprinted on the sidewall of a tire represents the speed rating of the tire. Each letter indicates the top recommended speed for the tire under controlled conditions. The following is a list of common speed ratings:

N=87 mph,	140km/h
U=124 mph,	200km/h
P=93 mph,	150km/h
H=130 mph,	210km/h
Q=99 mph,	160km/h
V=149 mph,	240km/h
R=106 mph,	170km/h
W=168 mph,	270km/h
S=112 mph,	180km/h
Y=186 mph,	300km/h
T=118 mph,	190km/h
Z=149 mph,	240km/h and over

This new 17-inch tire has the same overall diameter as the factory 16-inch, but it offers a lower sidewall profile and wider track. Secure the vehicle with a jack and jack stands before removing the stock rubber and steel. Bolt on the new wheels and tighten the lugs. After all four corners are complete, drop the PT on the ground and torque the lugs to 100 ft-lbs.

PROJECT 5 ★ *Performance Spring Installation*

Time: **5 hours**

Tools: **Pry bar, spring compressor, socket set, jack, jack stands, tape measure, utility knife**

Talent: ★★★

Tab: **$350**

Parts: **Springs**

Tip: **Complete each corner before moving to the next. Have wheel alignment performed when you're done.**

Benefit: **Better road manners, improved handling, competition appearance**

In stock configuration (even the GT model), all PTs have a disproportionate amount of fender-well gap (the space measured from the top of the tire to the apex of the fender opening). By installing performance or lowering springs, you can improve the handling and appearance of the vehicle in one inexpensive shot.

There is a primary difference in terms of function between performance and lowering springs. Performance springs are engineered to improve the handling capabilities of a PT, with the bonus of an improved appearance. Lowering springs are designed to reduce the ride height of the PT and any performance benefit is a plus.

Performance springs are designed to properly and safely lower the PT's center of gravity by using progressive spring rates. They reduce squat during acceleration, body roll in the turns, and nose dive under braking. Upon installation, your PT should become exceptionally stable and secure under a much wider range of conditions.

Professionals make these installations look easy. However, PT Cruisers are some of the easiest vehicles on which to perform a spring swap. While this job may be a bit too difficult for some, it can be done with common tools and a spring compressor, which can be rented from most automotive parts stores or equipment rental companies. When using a spring compressor, be careful to not allow the spring to bind or compress unevenly. A lot of energy is stored in a compressed spring and if it lets go, it can do some serious damage to you and your car.

Whenever working under your PT Cruiser, always use a solid, flat surface. Concrete is preferred.

Asphalt can get soft and unstable as it heats up and become a less than sufficient working surface.

Begin the installation by taking measurements while the vehicle is on a flat surface. Measure the distance from the bottom of the tire to the apex of the fender-well opening on all four corners. You can do this again after the installation to document the change in your car's ride height. Loosen the wheels' lug nuts. Next, raise the car into the air using an approved lift or jack, support the car with jack stands, and remove the wheels.

We'll start with the front springs. Safely support the vehicle and remove the front wheels. Remove the three 13-millimeter bolts that attach the top of the shock to the chassis.

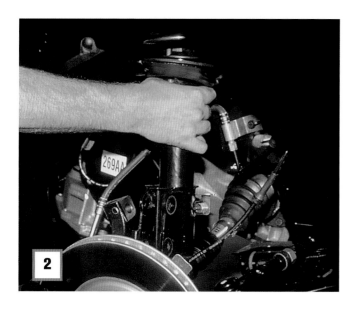

2. Next, remove the two 20-millimeter nuts on the bolts that attach the strut to the lower control arm.

3. To remove the bolts it may be necessary to tap them out with a hammer. Remove the grounding strap that attaches the chassis to the strut. The strut assembly can now be removed from the vehicle.

4. Mark the alignment of the top hat with the other parts of the strut assembly. This will simplify assembly of the strut once the new springs are installed.

5. Use a spring compressor to compress the factory spring. Remove the bolt that attaches the top hat to the strut and remove the top hat.

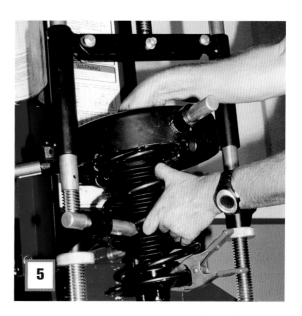

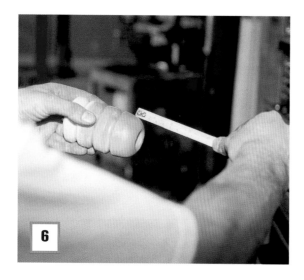

6

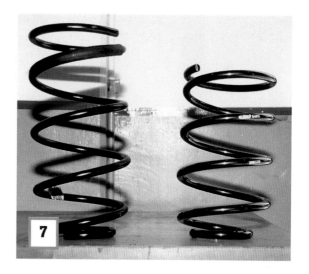

7

Once the protective boot has been removed, the bump stop will be exposed. Remove the bump stop and trim approximately 1 inch as shown. Reinstall the bump stop in its original location.

The new performance springs (in this installation Eibach ProKit springs were used) are noticeably shorter than the factory springs. Expect about a two-inch drop.

8

Install the new spring onto the strut and use the spring compressor to compress it enough to allow installation of the top hat. Once the top hat has been installed, decompress the spring. Now reinstall the strut into the vehicle by reversing steps 1 through 3.

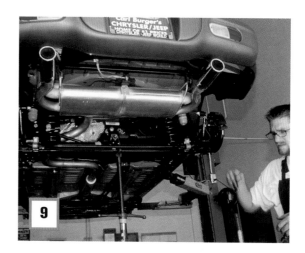

9

To replace the rear springs, first raise the vehicle and use jack stands to support the vehicle by a location other than the rear axle. Do not lower the jack, but use the jack to support the rear axle during disassembly.

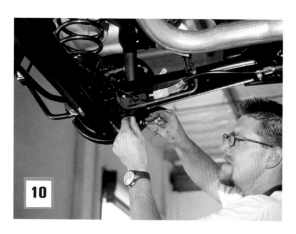

10

Remove the 16-millimeter bolts that attach the rear shocks to the rear axle on both sides. Remove the bolt that connects the anti-roll bar to the end link on each side.

Install the bump stops back into their original locations.

Now slowly lower the floor jack until the rear axle drops down enough to allow removal of the springs. Remove the bump stops located immediately outside of the spring on each side and trim the last section of the bump stops.

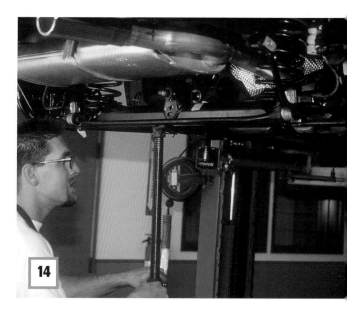

The rear spring is progressively loaded and, again, shorter than the stock spring.

Install the new springs in place and raise the rear axle with the floor jack. Reconnect the anti-roll bar end links, the bottom strut bolts, and reinstall the wheels. Lower the PT to the ground.

PROJECT 6 ★ *Air-Ride Suspension Installation*

Time: 6-8 hours

Tools: Pry bar, jack stands, power drill, socket set

Talent: ★ ★ ★

Tab: $1,850 – $2,100

Parts: Springs

Tip: If a lift is not accessible, work on a concrete surface. Do not work under a vehicle elevated on dirt, grass, or asphalt.

Benefit: Variable ride height

There are a growing number of enthusiasts who desire that ultra-low, street-custom look, but also need to retain the vehicle's streetability. With ground-scraping ride heights come a fear of speed bumps, potholes, and a host of other common daily driving obstacles. This is where air suspension can be the logical answer.

Air-ride suspension packages offer versatility by fitting the rear axle with a pair of Firestone air bags. These tubes of industrial-strength rubber are reinforced air bladders that expand and contract, depending on air pressure. They replace the coil springs and are fed by a high-pressure air line. Pump in the air, the rear lifts; then let out the air and it drops.

Air bags are not used for the front suspension because as the wheels turn, they twist the spring/damper assembly. This constant torsion can quickly destroy a rubber air bag. The solution is a machined aluminum air cylinder with an internal damper. It looks like an oversized strut and bolts up to the factory mounting points. Like the air bags, a high-pressure line feeds the air cylinder, then raises and lowers the suspension with the push of a button. Be aware that there are air-ride lowering kits without a damper up front, using nothing but the air spring. These are more for show and not for daily driven PTs. High-quality air cylinders have internal dampers to control oscillation and allow your PT to handle with relative ease.

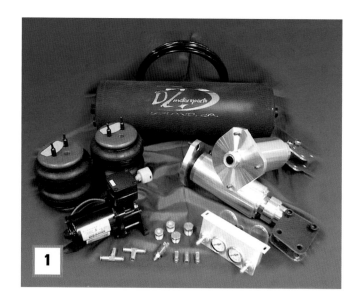

A complete kit should contain all of the necessary components: air tank, compressor, rear air bags, front air cylinders, control switches, gauges, and all the required plumbing hardware.

We start at the rear, where we will replace the coil springs with air bags in the same location. To do this, you must first elevate the vehicle and support it with jack stands. Safety Note: Support the vehicle by placing the jack stands under the jacking points, not the rear axle. Use a floor jack to support the axle. Unbolt the Watts linkage (this is the center pivot bar that attaches the center of the rear axle to the chassis) by removing the 15-millimeter nut and tapping out the bolt. Next, unbolt (15 millimeters) the rear anti-roll bars. Unbolt the shocks (16 millimeters) from the lower mounting points and gently lower the rear axle. This will help remove the stored energy in the springs. Now the springs can be easily removed. Springs store a lot of energy, so take precautions not to direct the spring toward you. You may want to keep the factory springs in case you'd like to reinstall them in the future.

The Firestone air bag is a simple device. It is constructed in a fashion similar to a tire.

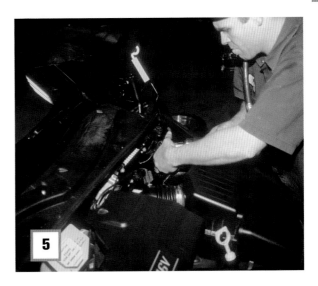

In the front, the strut is removed by removing the three 13-millimeter nuts from the mount in the fender well and from the 20-millimeter attachment points on lower suspension link. There is no need to remove the factory springs from the strut assembly; the air cylinder is a direct replacement for both. The entire installation is very straightforward, with all components fitting the factory locations.

The air bag mounts to custom steel buckets and it is put in place between the rear axle and the chassis. Once the air bag is in place, jack up the axle assembly and bolt the shock to the lower mounting points. Reattach the anti-roll bar.

The Drop Zone air cylinder is visible through the factory strut mount. The high-pressure air line mounts here and hints at the special suspension set-up.

The air cylinder bolts to the front upright. It is a serious piece of machined componentry and looks beautiful, especially compared to the strut/coil spring assembly it replaces.

The control center for the Drop Zone air suspension consists of two switches, one for the front and one for the rear, to control the attitude of the PT. This view is of the rear of the control center. On the front, dual gauges monitor air pressure.

9

With the suspension kit installed, the PT takes on a whole new look . . . low and mean. The PT benefits from improved aesthetics and may improve daily use handling. However, this is not a high-performance application and should not be treated as such. When the road gets rough, the air ride suspension allows a PT to navigate over obstacles with confidence and style. When compared to conventional fixed-height lowering kits, an air suspension offers convenient flexibility that makes owning a lowered PT a reasonable, real-world option. Going low in the front and high in the rear presents yet another option.

10

11

PROJECT 7 ★ *Anti-Roll Bars*

Time: **3 hours**

Tools: **Vise, Channel Lock pliers, socket set, floor jack, jack stands or ramps**

Talent: ★ ★ ★

Tab: **$250**

Parts: **Anti-roll bars, bushings**

Tip: **Install and settle at ride height**

Benefit: **Better road manners, improved handling**

One of the most significant PT chassis improvements you can make is to reduce the car's body roll during cornering. The main function of this process is to slightly reduce the independence of the suspension via anti-roll bars for front and rear.

In plain terms, anti-roll bars are marginally flexible steel bars that connect the chassis of a vehicle to both sides of front or rear suspension, thus linking the action and reaction of the suspension. The concept is to offer a semi-pliable triangulation of the suspension, limiting excessive movement in the process.

In theory, the physics of anti-roll bars are simple. The job of the component is to stabilize the stiffness by which the suspended structure (sprung mass) of a vehicle is connected to the unsuspended wheel/tire/axle/hub combination (unsprung mass). The extent to which the unsprung mass moves independently of its opposing counterpart and the sprung mass can be increased or decreased by the length and diameter of the anti-roll bar. In essence, stiffer anti-roll bars flex less, and cause the vehicle's chassis to be less affected by the lateral forces working against it while in motion. By connecting the suspension members and increasing the spring rate when they act counter to each other, the chassis remains flatter to the driving surface. Softer anti-roll bars permit more suspension motion when affected by the same lateral force.

There are advantages and disadvantages to strengthening or weakening the relationship between unsprung and sprung mass movement. In the most popular case, stiffer bars are fitted to reduce body roll and improve handling. Modifying anti-roll bar stiffness in the front or rear independently can further improve a vehicle's handling characteristics, tuning

oversteer and understeer, and quickening transitional response (the time it takes for a vehicle to return to neutral balance after encountering a corner).

Anti-roll bars are a relatively easy installation. Starting in front, safely lift and support the vehicle, or drive it up onto a pair of ramps designed to support a vehicle. The ramps allow the suspension to remain at the proper ride height, which is necessary when tightening things up after the installation. Remove the 15-millimeter anti-roll bars' end link bolts, nuts, and insulators from the control arms. With the anti-roll bar supported, remove the clamp bolts and clamps. The factory anti-roll bar is now free of the vehicle.

Any high-quality performance anti-roll bar kit will include new bushings, usually made of molded urethane. Install the bushings onto the new front anti-roll bar. Be sure to grease the bushings—this will help prevent squeaks as the new anti-roll bar does its job.

To complete the front anti-roll bar install, first loosely attach the new bar by the frame bushings. This will give you just enough slack to make minor adjustments, if necessary. Make sure the openings of the bushings are pointed down when installed. This will help trapped road debris to work its way out. When this is complete, tighten the frame-mount bushings.

To prevent any possibility of the suspension binding up, it is important to tighten the mounting points of an anti-roll bar when the PT is sitting at ride height. This is easy to do if the car is on ramps, and a little more challenging if you're using jack stands. Align the end links and anti-roll bar at a 90-degree angle to each other and bolt everything

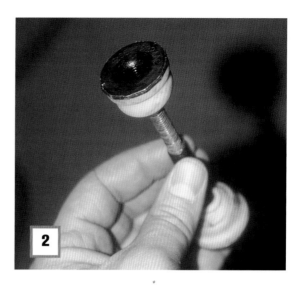

1 and 2: Start in front by removing the anti-roll bar end links. The upper end is essentially a thick washer that can be held with Channel Lock pliers. Removal and installation of anti-roll bars is easiest with suspension at ride height.

together. If you're using jack stands, lower the car to the ground. Bounce the vehicle to settle the suspension, then reach under the car and tighten the end links until the bushings are a bit larger in diameter than the supporting washers.

Replacing the rather thin (16 millimeters) factory rear anti-roll bars will pay substantial dividends. For street applications, a 22-millimeter aftermarket bar is ideal. Replacing the rear anti-roll bars is as easy as the front bar swap (if not easier). Install Tip: When unbolting the rear end links, you can avoid tire interference by raising the vehicle so the bolt can be easily removed.

Unbolt the bar from the end links and suspension beam attachment points. Lift the bar away from the suspension beam. You will need to expand the bushing mounts. Securing the mounts in a vise and prying the safety tabs open can do this. Place the new bushing in the mount and thoroughly grease it. There is no need to bend the safety tabs back because the mounts will be through-bolted.

Finish by tightening the connection points. The rear anti-roll bar should not be tightened until the PT has been set back at ride height and settled. Once that is

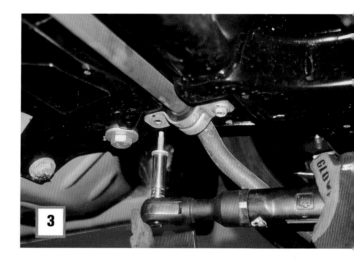

Loosen the frame-mount bushings before doing the end links, but don't remove them until the end links have been removed. The OEM urethane bushings are not reused.

done, complete the tightening. Go back and recheck all your connection points, including the wheel lug nuts.

Performance anti-roll bars will create a much more confident ride and increase driver feedback. You will feel the difference the first time around the block. However, bars that are too thick will make driving more challenging and can even be dangerous for street use. The ideal street size seems to be 26-millimeter front and 22-millimeter rear.

The replacement bushings should be of a higher grade of urethane than the original black factory bushings. Good-quality urethane bushings (this one is red) have molded pockets to hold grease. This is a lubricant used to keep the bushings quiet. DO NOT forget to grease the bushings, and use the grease liberally.

5 and 6: Attach the new bar by the frame bushings first, loosely, which gives you the slack to make adjustments. Make sure the bushing's opening is pointed down when installed so any trapped road crud can work its way out. When tightening the end links of an anti-roll bar, it is imperative the PT is sitting at ride height, or the suspension may bind.

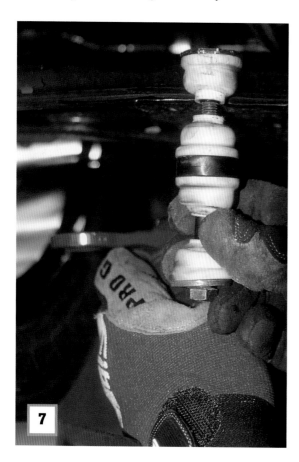

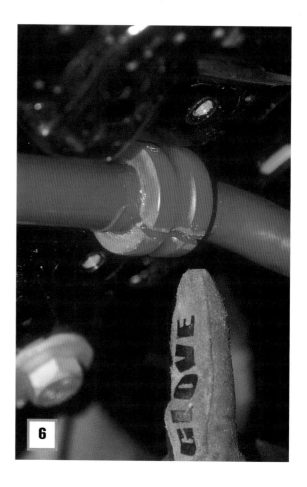

To connect the end links, align them as pictured. The end link and anti-roll bar should be at 90 degrees to each other. Bounce the vehicle to settle the suspension. Tighten the end links until the bushings are a bit larger in diameter than the washer supporting them. Tighten the frame-mount bushings second.

The rear bar comes out as easily as the front. When unbolting the rear end links, it helps to raise the vehicle so the bolt can be removed without tire interference.

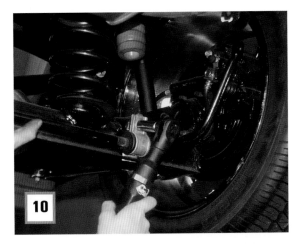

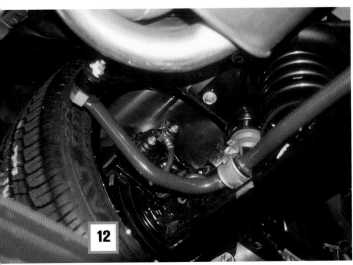

10: The beam-mount bushing must be disassembled to swap the bushing. It comes out with the OEM anti-roll bar.

11: Secure the bushing mounts in a vise and pry the safety tab open. You don't need to bend the tab back down because that mount will be through-bolted when reinstalled.

12: Here, the new bar is installed and tightened. The rear bar should not be tightened until the car has been set back at ride height and settled.

PROJECT 8 ★ *Performance Air Filter Replacement*

Time: 10 minutes

Tools: Flathead screwdriver

Talent: ★

Tab: $35

Parts: Air filter

Tip: The hardest part is lifting the hood

Benefit: The easiest 2-horsepower gain you'll ever install; it may be the last air filter you ever need to buy

Housed within that massive, molded plastic box and taking up a disproportionate amount of room under the hood is a zigzag shape of paper in a rubber frame. This is commonly referred to as an air filter. Its purpose is to help prevent dirt, dust, and other contaminants from reaching your PT's intake system.

With every mile you put on your PT, the air filter collects the airborne junk that passes through the air intake port. As the filter gets more and more clogged, airflow is restricted and power and fuel economy suffer. The factory recommends changing the air filter every 30,000 miles. This will help keep the engine running the way Chrysler intended. If you want a little more power and a filter that needs replacing after a reported one million miles, a simple K&N filter change is all that needs to be done.

A K&N filter flows about 60 percent more air over the factory paper element and traps more contaminants to boot. To install this wonder of wonders, start by simply opening the hood. The air box is located on the driver's side of the engine compartment. Unlatch the securing clips located on the top of the air box. Lift the cover and remove the factory filter. Drop in the K&N filter, then latch the air box top. Lower and secure the hood. You're done.

Once you lift the hood, the factory air filter housing is located on your right (otherwise known as the vehicle's left).

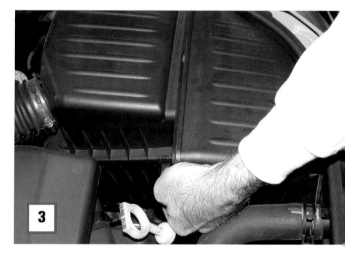

2: K&N makes a highly superior air filter. For non-GT models, the part number you'll need is 33-2153. K&N also makes a high-quality oil filter (HP-1002).

3: Unlatch the upper air box attachment points located on each side of the box.

4: Remove the top of the air box, lift out the paper filter, and install the new performance air filter, making sure the filter is oriented correctly relative to the airflow on its way to the engine. Install the box top in reverse order.

PROJECT 9 ★ *Ignition Upgrade*

Time: 30-60 minutes

Tools: Screwdrivers and socket set

Talent: ★★

Tab: $300

Parts: Plasma Booster

Tip: Work on a cool engine

Benefit: Horsepower

One area under the hood that has traditionally fallen short on performance for most vehicles is the ignition system's lack of potential energy supply. This can cause horsepower to be deficient, especially under prolonged demand. This is magnified when a PT is outfitted with aftermarket performance components, such as forced induction systems and/or high-flow exhaust kits.

Recently innovations in ignition enhancements can provide as much as six additional horsepower to a basic model and as much as 10 more ponies to GT models. The Plasma Booster system from Ignition Solutions requires no line cutting or splicing and it can be installed in as little as 20 minutes.

This product works remarkably well. Even more noteworthy is how easy it is to install. On the PT, there is an open location on the firewall of the engine compartment that is the ideal location to mount the Plasma Booster box. The unit is held in place with industrial-strength, double-sided adhesive strips. The wiring is run to the location where each connection will mate to the designated wire running in and out of the vehicle's control unit. Wire integration clips are used to marry the signals. No wires are directly cut, providing a clean, low-risk installation.

With no special installation skills required, even mechanically inexperienced PT Cruiser owners can do the job in only 30 minutes. In addition to producing horsepower, the product produces reduced emission levels and increased fuel mileage.

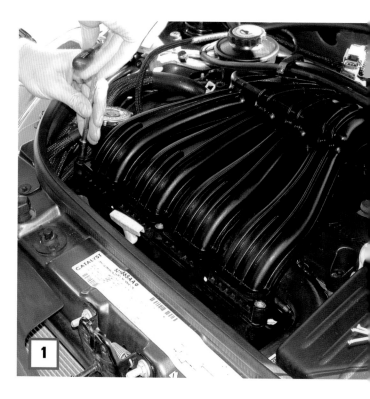

Start by performing the most difficult part of the install: removing the intake manifold by removing the five 8-millimeter nuts that connect the upper and lower intake manifold.

Attach the double-sided adhesive strips to the Plasma Booster box and mount in a clear area. For this application, a spot on the firewall proved to be an ideal location.

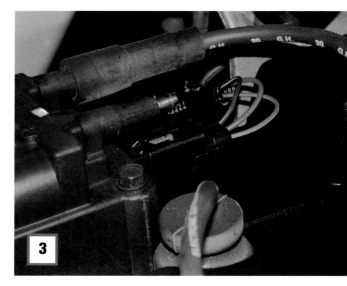

Disconnect the male to female connectors. One unclips, while the other requires a small socket.

Installation is made simple by the use of Quick-Slide connectors.

The wires from the Plasma Booster box simply plug into place. Consult the wiring diagram to ensure proper placement. The third wire connects to ground. Once this is complete, you're done. Use a few tie wrap straps to neatly secure the wiring if necessary. Now reinstall the air intake and test it.

Following the easy-to-read wire diagram (included), attach the connectors to the designated wires.

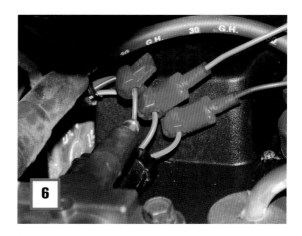

PROJECT 10 ★ *Performance Air Induction*

Time: 1 hour

Tools: Phillips screwdriver, socket set

Talent: ★

Tab: $225

Parts: Intake system kit

Tip: Work on a cool or cold engine

Benefit: 3-7 horsepower gain

One of the easiest ways to add acceleration and improve throttle response to non-turbo PTs is to install a cold-air and/or high-flow air intake system.

The term "cold-air intake" is an often misused or overused description—a marketing term for snorkel-style units that draw air into the engine's throttle body. The purpose of a performance induction system is to deliver one or a combination of higher volume, accelerated airflow, or cool air from outside the engine compartment.

Calling some of these devices "cold air" can be a misnomer, because the air the tube draws upon is not any cooler than that of the factory intake. Many systems can claim to provide high-flow induction, as the aftermarket unit provides a larger capacity or supply of air over stock, but they will not necessarily provide air from a source where the temperatures are lower than the heat dissipated from the engine. If the tube is accessing cooler air from the cowl, fender well, air dam, or behind a headlight, then it can be labeled a cold-air intake system.

The reason performance air systems create horsepower is that cooler, denser air (and more of it) improves the oxygen content of the cylinder charge for more powerful fuel combustion. In some cases, routing the intake tube to grab exterior air can be a difficult proposition. It is vital to locate the inlet to a cooler section of the engine bay. Tubing dimension is also a concern—if the ID (inside diameter) is too large, airflow velocity suffers. Look for a 1/4- to 1/2-inch ID increase over stock, as well as a straighter air path and smooth inner tube walls.

There are various air-intake snorkels designed for the PT Cruiser. Better-breathing filter makers like K&N Engineering have their under-hood options, and a wealth of other manufacturers have engineered other performance intake concepts.

Remove the factory intake snorkel all the way up to the mass air sensor. Be sure to pop out the intake air-temp sensor and the one fitting sprouting from beneath.

Most aftermarket intake systems replace the OEM intake's slip-fit mass air attachment with a rubber collar and two hose clamps. These are easy to install and are a good fit.

Install the vacuum hose and air-temp sensor in the new intake tube, and you're in business.

A popular question is which is better: foam or cotton-gauze filter elements. Cotton units are considered a better filter device, because there is no way for a synthetic material to be as complex a particle trap as a natural cotton fiber. The other side argues that synthetic elements or foam filters, impregnated with a sticky treatment such as a heavy oil or spray-on resin-based fluid, allow for improved airflow at high rpm.

In the end, it all comes down to delivering the goods. Claims of 10 percent increases in horsepower and torque are difficult to believe. A more realistic number is a 3 to 7 percent horsepower gain.

It is wise to remember that you get what you pay for. Be prepared to pay more for a brand name. More attractive parts are not always the most effective—performance is completely colorblind. Costs for intake systems can range from $90 to $300.

Auxiliary intake systems are among the easiest aftermarket performance parts to install. There is not much more involved than the removal of a few nuts and bolts, removing the factory snorkel hardware, and installation of the new unit per manufacturers' instructions. Installation can be accomplished with the use of common tools.

Start by lifting the hood. Remove the oversized factory air box by loosening the ring clamps that connect the air tubing to the throttle body. Release the pair of clips that hold the air filter housing cover. This provides access to the air filter. When the air filter element is removed, the entire air box can be lifted up and pulled from the engine compartment. It is held in place by positioning pins, so only a moderate amount of force is necessary to remove the box.

Once the factory air box and related tubing have been removed, there is a rather large hole in the left side of the engine compartment. Fill this void with a simple performance air-intake system. Simply fit the ring clamps over the rubber tubing. Most PT Cruiser performance air-intake systems install using pre-existing mounting points and should have the fittings to correspond with proper vacuum and air temperature sensors.

For the most part, a performance air-intake system will require a small time investment and will pay remarkable horsepower dividends.

PROJECT 11 ★ *Supercharger Install*

Time: 8-12 hours

Tools: Power drill, socket set, torque wrench

Talent: ★★★★

Tab: $3,150 – $3,500

Parts: Jackson Racing Supercharger Kit

Tip: Follow the instruction sheet to the letter. Allow more time than you think. Label all the attachment hoses and lines for easier recognition.

Benefit: Power, torque, acceleration

Forced induction is one of the most popular and potent ways to increase the horsepower of a PT Cruiser. There are two basic means of forced induction, supercharging and turbocharging. Both will provide many benefits, such as vastly improved acceleration. Both are relatively expensive. Of the two, a supercharger kit is easier to install.

There is a good deal of misinformation regarding supercharging; the worst is that supercharging will easily damage the engine. However, supercharging does not significantly increase the stress and strain on the engine's internal components. There can be problems, however, if detonation occurs. Detonation occurs when the gases in the combustion chamber are under severe pressure and heat. These factors cause the mixture to auto-ignite at points other than the spark plug ignition. When this happens, pressure waves radiate out and collide with the pressure waves from the spark plug ignition to create rapid pressure rises within the combustion chamber. Detonation can be avoided using one or all of the following: conservative boost pressure, intercooling, water injection, and high-octane fuel. Supercharging, when done properly, will not damage your engine.

The Jackson Racing system features an Eaton supercharger and a specially engineered intake manifold. Following installation instructions is vital to success. The design of a kit's instructions is equally as important as the kit's components.

This is a rather lengthy installation, so set aside at least a full day and perhaps an entire weekend of dedicated time. Begin by draining the coolant from the radiator. Next, unplug the air temperature sensor and remove (but do not discard) the plastic tunnel leading from the air box to the throttle body. Lift out the entire factory air box and filter assembly.

As you read through this book, you will notice that nearly everything that can be modified under the hood requires you to remove the upper intake manifold. Therefore, it makes sense to perform a number of installations in tandem (if possible). The supercharger install requires that the upper intake manifold be completely removed. Using a 10-millimeter socket, unbolt the throttle body, accelerator linkage, and the five 8-millimeter attachment points holding the upper intake manifold in place.

Some say supercharger, and others call it a blower. Whatever the terminology, this air spinner is a horsepower factory.

Drain the coolant into a container. After unplugging the air temperature sensor and removing the hard plastic pipe from the rear of the air box hose, remove the air box assembly. This will be reused later.

The ignition coil is located on top of the cam cover (also referred to as a valve cover). Unplug the spark plug wires from the coil and the two electrical terminal blocks. Unbolt the coil (10 millimeters) unit from the cover—it will be reinstalled later. You will find a cast-aluminum bracket on the back of the head. Remove it. Remove the power steering reservoir and cruise control controller (10 millimeters). This will be relocated later.

Remove the upper radiator hose and thermostat housing from the water neck (10 millimeters). Like other factory components, these too will be used later in the assembly process. Unplug the fuel injector wiring harness.

Unbolt and unplug all the various attachments to the intake manifold. Unbolt the upper intake manifold and remove it. Remember that following instructions is vital to success.

The fuel rail and fuel injectors are located on the lower intake manifold; these must also be removed (8 millimeters). Remove the lower intake manifold by removing the oil dipstick and its housing. Like the upper intake, there are five 8-millimeter fasteners that hold the lower intake in place. Once these are removed, the lower intake can be lifted off.

Disconnect the alternator and push it into the gap between the firewall and the rear crossmember (located beside the heat shield). Remove the upper alternator bracket. It will require you to slightly

Unbolt and remove the coil from the top of the valve cover. This too will be used later. Remove the cast-aluminum support bracket from the back of the cylinder head.

Remove the power steering reservoir. If you have cruise control, remove the controller. This will be relocated later.

Remove the upper radiator hose from the thermostat neck. Save this part, too. Remove the thermostat housing.

Unplug the fuel injector wiring harness.

tweak the exhaust heat shield in order to access the mounting bolts.

The upper alternator bracket needs a small modification to extend its length. Drill two 27/64-inch holes using the provided drill bit following the template included in the kit. Install the extended-adjustment nut onto the upper alternator mount.

Unbolt the ground strap located on the passenger side of the head. Install an 8-millimeter x 40-millimeter stud (included in the kit) in this hole and two more studs in the threaded holes on each side of the original ground hole. A rear support shelf is installed onto these studs and secured with the 8-millimeter flanged nuts. Now you're ready to install the belt drive bracket onto the passenger end of the support shelf. Be sure to leave these bolts only finger-tight at this time. Reinstall the coil onto the support shelf.

You're not ready to remove and relocate engine appendages yet. Remove the coolant reservoir from the firewall and relocate it using a supplied bracket. Install the new lower intake manifold onto the engine. Be sure all the proper gaskets are in place before securing the new lower half in place. Install the fuel injectors and fuel rail. Install the new upper manifold/supercharger assembly onto the lower manifold. Torque the 8-millimeter flanged nuts to 16 ft-lbs.

Now that the supercharger is installed, reinstall all of the affected components in the reverse order of their removal. Check to make sure everything has been bolted back on, plugged in, tightened, filled, adjusted, and replaced correctly. Don't forget things like engine coolant and power steering fluid.

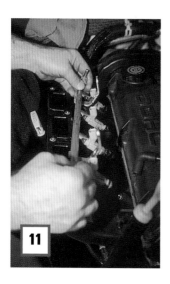

Remove and save the fuel rail and injectors. Remove the lower intake manifold.

Remove the alternator and push it back into the gap between the firewall and the rear crossmember, located next to the heat shield. Remove the upper alternator bracket. You may have to bend the exhaust heat shield to access the mounting bolts.

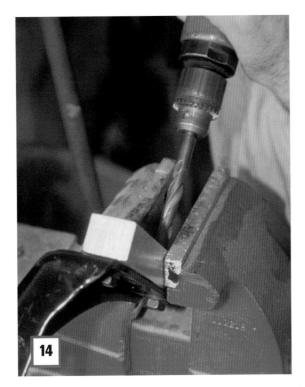

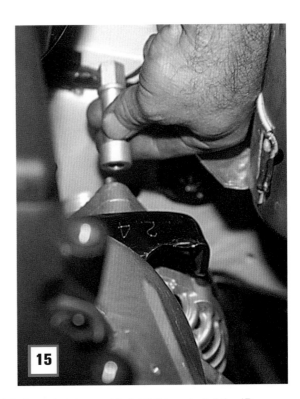

Modify the upper alternator bracket by drilling two 27/64-inch holes using the provided drill fixture. Install the JR extended-adjustment nut onto the upper alternator mount.

Unbolt the ground strap from the passenger side of the head. Install studs in the holes on each side of the original ground hole. Install the rear support shelf onto these studs and secure with the 8-millimeter flanged nuts.

Install the belt drive bracket onto the passenger end of the support shelf. Leave these bolts loose. Install the coil onto the support shelf as shown.

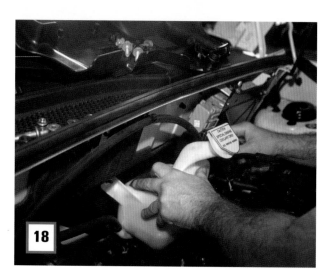

Remove the coolant reservoir from the firewall. Relocate using the supplied bracket.

Install the new lower intake manifold onto the engine.

Install the injectors and fuel rail in the reverse order of their removal. Install the new upper manifold/supercharger assembly onto the lower manifold.

Attach the drive belt and tighten.

PROJECT 12 ★ *Turbocharging*

Time: 18-24 hours

Tools: Floor jack or lift, jack stands, power drill, socket set, torque wrench

Talent: ★★★★★

Tab: $3,500 – 4,500

Tip: Bribe a friend to help you and put him up for the weekend. Put pizza delivery on speed dial. Allow extra time to tune the system after installation.

Benefit: Massive horsepower potential

The previous pages demonstrated how to add power by installing a supercharger. Now it's time to explore other options—namely, an aftermarket turbocharger.

The difference between supercharging and turbocharging is simple. The crankshaft drives a supercharger via a belt. A turbocharger is driven by exhaust pressure passing through a turbine. There are positive and negative aspects to each type of installation. Superchargers provide instantaneous power because they don't have to spool up to speed as turbochargers do. The turbo, on the other hand, doesn't suffer from complex belt assemblies and offers potential for larger power increases.

This procedure will provide an overview of an average turbo installation and give a general primer on turbocharging basics. This is by no means a complete installation guide. Many more pages would be needed for that. This will, however, give you a very good understanding of what you're in for before attempting to install the average turbocharger on your PT Cruiser.

For this installation, the Hahn turbo kit was used. This is a fairly straightforward installation. The turbo bolts to the provided exhaust manifold, which replaces the factory manifold. The idea is to route the exhaust through the turbo, then out the exhaust system. The exhaust pressure spins the turbine impeller at high speeds (approximately 100,000 rpm) and the impeller drives the compressor turbine on the other end of the turbocharger. The compressor forces air into the engine via large, red silicone hoses.

The purpose of turbocharging is to add power. The turbo only supplies more air to the combustion chamber. More air means you can convert more fuel into energy, so it is necessary to provide the engine with additional fuel. To accomplish this, an auxiliary or higher volume fuel pump is often necessary. In most cases, the high-pressure fuel pump is installed somewhere between the fuel tank (that has an internal fuel pump) and the in-line fuel regulator. The factory fuel regulator is scrapped in place of a new, adjustable regulator that can provide more accurate fuel flow to the injectors under the higher demand created by the greater velocity and volume of air entering the intake system.

One of the more intimidating procedures within the turbocharger install is tapping into the oil pan as an oil return line for the turbo unit. A fitting is

Included in the kit is the turbocharger, exhaust manifold, fuel regulator, air cleaner, and necessary tubing.

attached to the oil pressure-sending unit on the engine block. A line is mounted to this fitting and oil is fed to the turbo. After lubricating the impeller shafts, it flows down the return line to the oil pan and is reintroduced to the engine oiling system. This is where it gets tricky, as the oil pan does not have a pass-through or hole for the return line fitting. This makes a modification necessary. With the oil pan removed, a hole is drilled in the side. The hole is threaded with a tap and a fitting is installed. Though it seems intimidating, it is not a difficult procedure if the instructions are followed carefully. The reason you want to remove the oil pan to perform the drilling is to prevent metal shavings or particles from being introduced to the oil.

To remove the oil pan, drain the oil and remove the oil filter. There is a structural collar that needs to be removed to allow access to lower the pan. Remove

The Hahn turbo kit supplies a high-pressure fuel pump and adjustable pressure regulator. The Hahn fuel pump works in conjunction with the factory pump and supplies more fuel to the new regulator. The regulator is used to adjust the amount of fuel being delivered by the injectors.

the lateral bending brace and the lower torque strut. The flywheel inspection cover must also be removed.

There are thirteen 10-millimeter bolts that hold the pan onto the engine. Once all are removed, the pan should be free. If it is stuck, tap on the pan with a rubber mallet to break the gasket bead. With the pan off, but before drilling for the oil return line, remove the oil screen and pickup tube. After drilling the oil

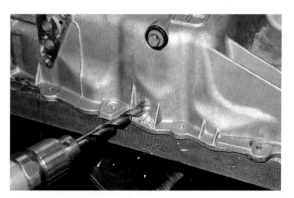

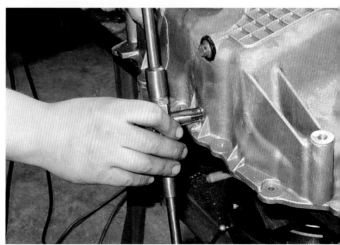

A turbo will spin at very high speeds, and therefore requires lubrication to avoid possible destruction. The engine also needs lubrication, and the oiling system can be tapped for turbo purposes. A fitting is attached to the oil pressure-sending unit on the engine block. A line is mounted to this fitting and oil is fed to the turbo. After lubricating the impeller shafts, it flows down the return line to the oil pan and is reintroduced to the engine oiling system.

Remove the oil pan and drill a hole in the pan's side.

The hole is threaded with a tap and a fitting is installed.

At this point, the turbo can be lubricated but the hoses that will route the compressed air from the turbocharger to the engine have yet to be installed. The Hahn kit is not intercooled, so the routing is simple. Large-diameter silicone hoses connect to the compressor outlet on the turbo and to the throttle body. These run down under the engine and back to the throttle body. To make the installation easy, keep all the hose clamps loose while all the hose ends are being connected. After the entire chain of hoses is properly fitted together, tighten all the connecting points.

Clean air is vital to the safe and efficient operation of any turbo unit. The supplied air filter is mounted to the compressor inlet with an air temperature sensor attached to the air filter.

return fitting, thoroughly clean the pan. This will help ensure that all metal shavings are removed and are not left to run throughout your engine.

Once you've completed the turbo oil return fitting, apply a bead of gasket sealer to the cylinder block and oil pump assembly joint at the oil pan flange. Install a fresh oil pan gasket and place the pan into position. Insert the oil pan bolts finger-tight. Tighten the bolts, working side-to-side from the center forward and back. Snug the bolts with a torque wrench to 105 in-lbs.

All turbocharger packages should come with a new exhaust manifold. This requires that the factory exhaust manifold be removed and discarded (save the item for future needs). The exhaust manifold is secured to the engine block with ten 10-millimeter fasteners. There are also three 10-millimeter nuts that hold the exhaust down pipe to the manifold. All these are removed as well as the oxygen sensor (located on the right side of the manifold). Once the factory exhaust manifold is removed, the turbo exhaust manifold is secured in place. There is a specific tightening pattern that is preferred. Begin with the top center nuts, to the two most center lower nuts, to the top middle nuts, to the top corner nuts, and finally, the lower corner nuts. Tighten each evenly in the same

sequence to a final torque of 200 in-lbs of torque.

From this point, the turbo is installed onto the mounting points and exhaust manifold. The air-intake ducts are run, and heat shields are put in place. Each turbo kit requires this to be done in a different order, so consult the turbo manufacturers' notes and instructions.

DETONATION & INTERCOOLING

Like supercharging, turbocharging is not necessarily damaging to an engine. A well-designed kit may not harm or prematurely wear your engine. There can be problems if detonation occurs. Detonation can be avoided using one or all of the following: conservative boost pressure, intercooling, and high-octane fuel. Turbocharging, when done properly, will not damage your engine.

Intercooling helps prevent detonation by running the compressed air charge through a large heat exchanger before it reaches the throttle body. This effectively lowers the air temperature and reduces one of the potential causes of detonation, excessive heat. An intercooler will allow additional boost to be used. However, if boost pressures are conservative, an intercooler is not necessary.

PROJECT 13 ★ *Performance Exhaust System Install*

Time: **3 hours**

Tools: **Socket set, pry bar, jack, jack stands, creeper, mallet**

Talent: ★★

Tab: **$650**

Parts: **Muffler, tips, pre-bent tubing, U-bolts, gaskets**

Tip: **The higher and more stable you can get the vehicle, the easier the install**

Benefit: **Additional power and torque, performance exhaust tone, slightly improved fuel mileage**

Before reading on, walk out to your garage, open the overhead doors, jump in your PT, and start it up. Listen, hear the exhaust tone? No? Don't worry, nobody else can either. The fact is, Chrysler spent very little research and development money on the exhaust system to tune its tone and flow. Sure, the system is efficient and quiet, as is the system on the common, everyday Neon and Caravan. However, if you're reading this book, the last thing you want is common and everyday.

Aside from providing the sound of performance, an aftermarket exhaust system can also provide a few extra ponies and a bit more torque. Notice the key words here are *few* and *bit*. That's because exhaust

Although not a true dual exhaust system (which would be darn near impossible with the PT's in-line four-cylinder engine), this aftermarket system provides the look and sound of performance.

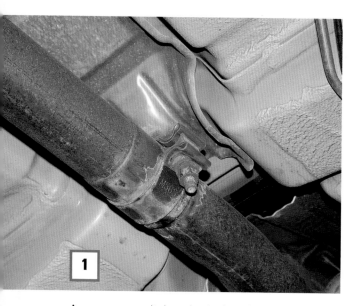

As you can see, it doesn't take long for the factory system to become road worn. If the bolts are difficult to remove, try a little liquid wrench to loosen any rust and corrosion.

A bit of light persuasion may be needed to loosen the factory exhaust sections.

systems, by themselves, will not deliver neck-snapping performance. Yet, by working in conjunction with a performance air intake, or better yet, a supercharger or turbocharger system, a better-flowing exhaust system is vital to realizing the full performance potential of the intake system.

The size and volume of the exhaust system makes it look and seem intimidating to work with. However, the truth is that installing a prefabricated system is not difficult. What makes the install problematic is the limited working space when a lift is not available.

The first step is to lift the PT to a working height or use a pit which you can drop into. Once under the vehicle, locate and remove the pair of rear rubber mounting hangers. Next, loosen the rear muffler clamp and remove the earth strap (10 millimeters) on the muffler. This is located at the chassis end. The muffler can now be removed. This may require a bit of force. Using a twisting motion while applying force helps free the muffler from the exhaust tubing.

The factory exhaust system consists of several pieces. For this install, the section from the catalytic converter back will be removed. The aftermarket system in this procedure is designed to be installed in a component-by-component manner. To finish removing the factory muffler and pipe, remove the mounting rubber on the center pipe and loosen the clamps.

Remove the pipe and both rubber hanger brackets.

You now have nothing aft of the factory catalytic converter. The catalytic converter (commonly referred to simply as "cat") serves as a vital component of your emission control system. DO NOT REMOVE THE CAT.

The process of installing the new performance system works primarily in reverse order of the removal of the factory system. First, install the hanger brackets and push the rubber insulators onto the brackets. Now you're ready to install the center exhaust section. Slide an exhaust clamp onto the front of the pipe and push the pipe onto the cat. Level the pipe before positioning the clamp so that it will snug down over the pipe extension of the cat and the sleeved pipe of the center section. Tighten the clamp firmly, but do not overtighten, because you will need a bit of slack to help level the rear sections.

Loosely attach the second section and connect to the aligned rubber mount. Do not forget to insert new gaskets. Next, loosely attach the rear section and mount to the rubber insulator. Again, be sure to insert new gaskets. Once all the sections are attached, push the entire system up into alignment and begin tightening the attachment points.

The critical point of this installation is the alignment of the rear exhaust exit points and the use of gaskets. The system used here was engineered to

Once the factory system is free from its attachment points, the entire system (from the cat back) can be removed as a single piece.

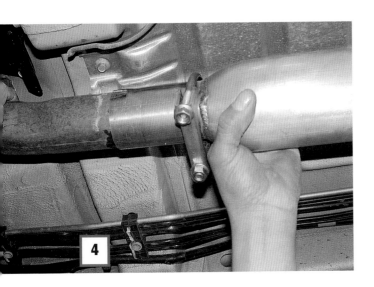

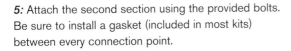

4: With the factory exhaust system out of the way, install the fore and aft hanger brackets. Slide a clamp over the front section and slip the pipe over the tail section of the cat.

5: Attach the second section using the provided bolts. Be sure to install a gasket (included in most kits) between every connection point.

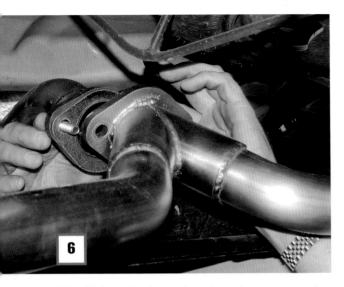

The third section diverts the exhaust into two rear exit points. Insert the gasket and bolt the flanges together.

use the factory hanger-attachment points, making the install much easier.

Many professional exhaust shops can also fabricate custom systems for specific needs. The advantages or disadvantages vary by the expertise of the shop and technicians, so, your results will vary. Be aware that bigger pipe is not always better. For PT Cruisers, 3-inch tubing provides more potential exhaust volume, but it does so at the price of correct back pressure, which slows down the velocity of the flow and can actually cost you horsepower. However, such large systems can be very beneficial to turbocharged and supercharged motors.

Lift the system and push the attachment arms into the hangers.

Follow the system from front to back and tighten all connection points.

PROJECT 14 ★ *Spark Plug Wire Replacement*

Time: 1 hour

Tools: Socket set

Talent: ★★

Tab: $99 – $275

Parts: Wires

Tip: Perform in conjunction with other ignition installs

Benefit: As much as a 2-horsepower gain

Over the past decade, performance spark plug wire products have flooded the automotive market. These are not new products; performance wires have been a staple of the V-8 performance world for 40 years. They have, however, found a new audience with the advent of small-engine performance.

To get a simple understanding of how ignition wires work, think of the wires as a common garden hose. The hose carries water from the faucet to the nozzle. The hose can carry a set volume of water based on its diameter. The larger the hose, the greater the volume of water it can carry (providing there is enough water pressure to fill the hose). There is a similar theory about ignition wires. A smaller-diameter wire, such as the Chrysler issued items, can transport small amounts of spark energy from the coil to the spark plugs. Increase the diameter, and you can increase the volume of energy delivered to the spark plugs. The question is, what is enough and what is too much?

There are many who believe that spark plug wires can provide no quantitative value, and that the energy delivered is all that is needed to initiate spark. Other experts stand by the belief that greater spark energy, delivered in short duration at hotter temperatures, will produce horsepower.

Generally, ignition wires need three milliseconds of spark duration to complete combustion. With a larger-diameter wire sending greater current flow, this duration time can be decreased to one to two milliseconds of spark duration. With capacitor-equipped wires, the spark duration can be cut to as little as four nanoseconds (one million times shorter), using only about two degrees of crankshaft rotation.

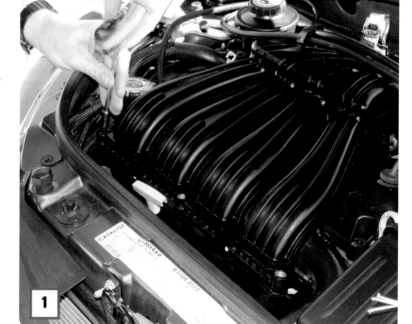

Start by removing the five 8-millimeter upper intake manifold connection points.

2

2 If you are performing only the spark plug wire swap (and perhaps an ignition box install), you can simply tilt the intake unit up as shown.

3: Disconnect and replace each plug wire, one by one.

To achieve power with a short spark life, you need to increase the plasma arc. Larger wires, such as those from MagnaCore and Vitek, supply more spark. Nology HotWires claim to increase spark energy by as much as 300 times over stock wires.

Swapping the factory wires for performance wires requires you to remove or tilt up the upper intake manifold. This is done by removing the five 8-millimeter bolts holding the upper intake manifold. When lifted out of place, the plug wires are fully exposed. Simply pull one wire at a time and replace with the new wire. When complete, reinstall the upper intake manifold.

3

Once the intake manifold is out of the way, changing the wires takes only a few minutes. The Nology wires have ground straps that can be connected to the cam cover bolts.

4

PROJECT 15 ★ *Engine Chrome*

Time: 3 hours

Tools: Socket set, screwdrivers

Talent: ★

Tab: $150

Parts: Chrome upper intake manifold, oil dipstick, transmission dipstick, caps, upper engine cover, air box cover, hood prop

Tip: Performing this modification with other under the hood installs will cut down on the overall time required to complete

Benefit: Superstar engine appeal, great for show

Performance is not, nor has it ever been, the PT Cruiser's strength. While engine performance is offered within these pages, many of the products devoted to the PT are cosmetic in nature. Dressing up an engine compartment is all about showing off. Under the bonnet of the PT sits a remarkably dull engine compartment. The space is at a premium, because nearly all available space is filled with some sort of device or component. The massive, molded plastic intake parts are plain and unattractive—clearly the result of a thought process stressing function over form.

Thankfully, the phenomenal enthusiast response to the crossover vehicle has provided owners with aftermarket products designed to provide new personality to nearly every area of the car, including under the hood.

The process of electroplating and repackaging factory original parts provides a factory fit and a measure of consumer confidence that is not usually found in early aftermarket product development.

The chrome package installation only requires that you replace the black molded components with plated parts. The upper engine cover is an easy replacement, but it will be the last item to be reinstalled. Lift off the existing unit and move on to the other components. Remove the factory air box by loosening the ring clamps that connect the air tubing to the throttle body. Release the pair of clips that hold the air filter housing cover. Pull the air box cover and replace with the chrome unit.

The next step requires replacement of the upper intake manifold. First, disconnect the electrical terminals leading from the IAC motor, throttle response sensor and absolute pressure sensor, air filter housing, accelerator cable, and cruise control cable. Remove the throttle body support bracket (13 millimeters) and hose leading to the EGR valve (10 millimeters). This is not

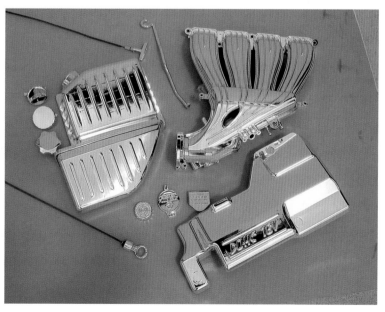

This is what you're going to install . . . cool.

2

Start by removing the air box cover.

3

You can also remove the upper engine cover.

as confusing as it sounds. IAC motor is an electrical connection plug located on the throttle body. The accelerator cable and cruise control cable are linked to the top of the throttle body and can be easily disconnected. Now, remove the five 8-millimeter bolts holding the upper intake manifold and lift it out of place. Fit the gaskets supplied in the package and install the new chrome-plated upper intake manifold. Once this is done, you will have completed the most time-consuming portion of the installation.

From this point forward, the rest of the project is a piece of cake. Replace the windshield washer bottle cap, radiator cap, power steering, and power brake caps. Pull the factory dipstick as well as the transmission fluid stick (automatic transmissions only), and replace with the chrome-plated counterparts.

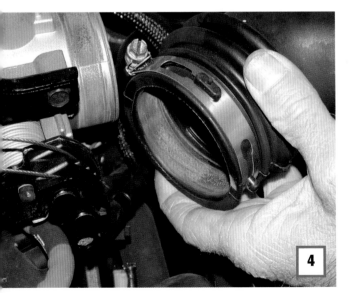

4

5

Remove all the connection points to the upper intake manifold (4). Remove the five bolts on the upper intake manifold (5).

The hood prop is on the driver's side of the engine compartment. Pop the foot of the prop through its factory-positioned hole, located near the junction of the inner fender panel, and replace it with the chrome-plated item.

The final piece of business requires removing the four 13-millimeter mounting tabs (which hold the top engine cover) from the old upper intake manifold. Line up the tabs on the exact same positions on the chrome upper intake manifold. Now, secure the chrome upper engine cover into position.

With all this done, stand back and admire a show-quality engine compartment.

Unbolt the throttle body from the upper intake manifold.

Lift off the upper intake manifold.

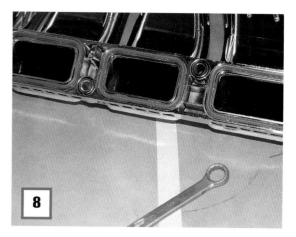

Fit the new gaskets into the chrome upper intake manifold.

Install the new upper intake manifold.

Replace the brake cylinder, coolant, washer tank, and power steering tank covers. The kit also includes a pressure-correct radiator cap.

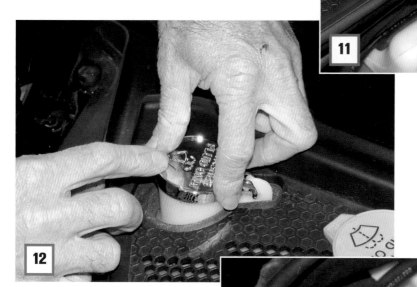

There are three upper engine cover mounting tabs that must be transferred from the black upper intake manifold to the chrome upper intake manifold.

With the mounting tabs in place, pop on the chrome upper engine cover.

The factory hood prop is on the left side (driver's) of the engine compartment. Push the foot of the prop through its mounting hole and replace it with the chrome-plated version.

The visual improvement is stunning.

65

PROJECT 16 ★ *Grille and Front Bumper Replacemen*

Time: 3 hours (after paint)

Tools: Socket set, pliers

Talent: ★ ★ ★

Tab: $1,200 (unpainted)

Parts: Front bumper/grille, reinforcement bar, simple hardware

Tip: Fit first, paint second, install third. Retain all the factory fasteners. Prepare a large, flat working area with blankets.

Benefit: Improved appearance

There is little denying the retro-hot rod styling the PT Cruiser brings to the street. For those who want to complete the package, the front bumper/grille assembly needs to be addressed.

While the components are large and bulky, making the project seem intimidating, the actual process is quite straightforward and easy. The installation begins by removing the hood. The hood is not vital to the install; removing it just gets it out of the way and will provide more workspace.

The factory grille and bumper unit can be removed using a 7-millimeter socket to remove the four nuts at the top of the grille. The grille can be pushed down and forward from the top. From here, remove the three nuts on each side of the factory splashguards and the edge of the bumper. Remove the three screws on the bottom of the scuff strip that fastens to the lower radiator support panel. Don't forget the two screws at the grille opening.

There are two nuts on each side of the bumper where it joins to the fenders. Remove them using a deep 10-millimeter socket. Carefully pull the splashguard back. This will enable you to reach in and disconnect the fog light connections. There is a speed clip by the left side fog light that also needs to be removed.

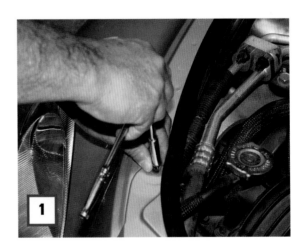

With the hood raised and propped, remove the four nuts located on the top of the grille.

Using the buddy system, remove the bumper cover from the PT. With the bumper and grille off the vehicle, the factory reinforcement bar is visible. While it is designed to enhance the safety of the original bumper, it is not compatible with the custom unit in this procedure. Therefore, remove the factory unit by

2

removing the 13-millimeter bolts. Save these bolts; they will be used later in the installation.

Place the new front fascia on a flat, protected surface alongside the factory unit. Remove all the hardware from the stock bumper and place each in the same location on the PTeazer front fascia. This is also the time to fit the fog lights in the new custom fascia.

Locate the new reinforcement bar in place on the front of the vehicle. Use the same 13-millimeter bolts removed from the factory bar. Attach the scuff strip to the new fascia using the fasteners from the original bumper.

Once all the mounting hardware has been transferred from the old to the new, position the new fascia to the vehicle using the exact same fasteners and mounting locations from the original bumper.

Once the nuts are removed, simply give a gentle lift on the grille and it pops out.

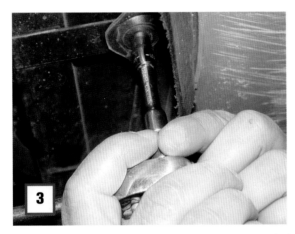

3

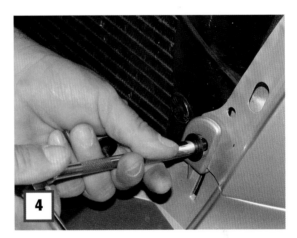

4

Remove the three nuts on each side of the factory splashguards and the edge of the bumper. Then remove the three nuts on the bottom of the scuff strip that fastens to the lower radiator support panel. Don't forget the two nuts at the grille opening.

5

From here, the bumper can easily be removed.

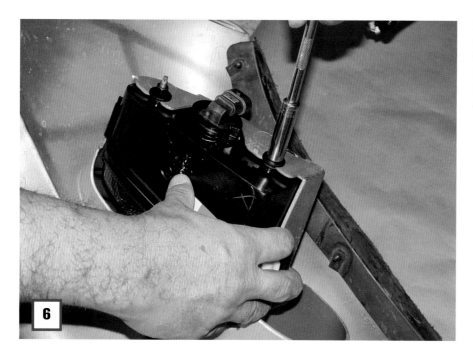

Remove the lower running lamps from the factory bumper and install in the same location on the new custom front fascia.

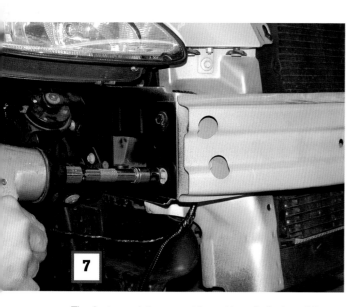

The factory reinforcement bar, although designed for safety, will not work with the custom unit. Remove the factory unit by removing the 13-millimeter bolts. Save these bolts; they will be used later in the installation.

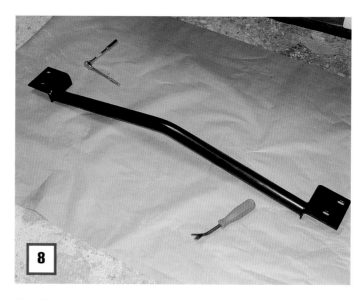

The PTeaser package includes a new reinforcement bar designed to accommodate the trick grille/bumper combo.

The new reinforcement bar installs using the factory mounting positions and 13-millimeter bolts.

When the new fascia is popped out of the mold, the mounting position holes are lightly sealed. Gentle pressure with a drill (3/32 bit) reopens the points.

Secure the new bumper fascia to the vehicle using the factory mounting positions and hardware.

The new custom grille is dropped into place and secured.

Recheck all the attachment points and close the hood gently to ensure that the alignment is right on.

PROJECT 17 ★ *Rear Roll Pan Install*

Time: 2-3 hours (after paint)

Tools: Power drill, screwdrivers, standard socket set, deep-set 10-millimeter socket

Talent: ★ ★ ★

Tab: $300

Parts: Roll pan kit, nuts and bolts (included)

Tip: Fit first, paint second, install third

Benefit: Improved appearance

One of the more engaging aspects of the PT Cruiser styling is how it can resemble a hot rod. Replacing the rear bumper with a rolled panel furthers this design notion. Chrysler's design and engineering team had to deal with issues far beyond aesthetics when the final rear-bumper shape was decided. Issues like crash safety and structural integrity took precedence over sensuous lines.

The automotive aftermarket stepped up to offer products that enhance the PT's appearance. Shortly after the release of the first PT Cruisers, several companies were developing a tucked rear-roll pan application. There are more than a dozen different aftermarket manufacturers offering these items in a choice of fiberglass, urethane, aluminum, or steel.

When making the decision to install a rear roll pan, there are considerations to make beyond the particular style of a given selection. Fit, finish, protection, durability, towing capability, and ease of installation are all serious factors.

Once you've made your selection, unless your PT is in full primer, you'll need to have the roll pan painted to match the rest of your Cruiser. Before sending off the part to the paint shop, take a few hours to remove the factory rear bumper and check-fit the new rear roll pan. It's a real bummer to go through the time and expense of having the item painted, only to find that the fit doesn't meet your standards. It is important to note that minor adjustments may be required prior to primer and paint. Openings for exhaust outlets may need to be cut and sanded smooth, for example. Some roll pans are designed to work with dual-exhaust setups. Make sure that your exhaust tips line up with the cutouts. You

don't want them touching the roll pan. If all is well, remove the factory rear bumper by first disconnecting the original back-up lamps and license plate light. It will be necessary to disconnect the wiring harness clips from the reinforcement bar. Next, open the liftgate and remove the scuff panel. This allows access to the bolts that hold the rear bumper bar in place. Once these are removed, it is a good idea to use jack stands to support the factory bumper.

Partially remove the rear wheel-well housing covers. Removing the tires and wheels can make access to these areas easier. Behind the plastic fender well covers you'll find 10-millimeter fasteners securing the bumper cover. Once these are removed, you

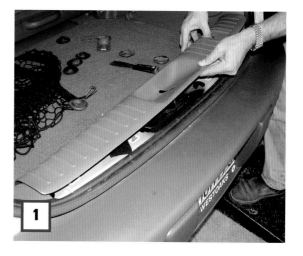

The installation of the new roll pan is straightforward. To gain access to the bumper bolts, open the liftgate and remove the plastic scuff panel.

Remove the bumper bolts hidden beneath the scuff panel. There are access holes that allow you to get a socket extension to the bolts.

and a helper can slide the original cover back until it is free of the vehicle.

Once the original bumper is removed, the factory reinforcement bar is exposed. Remove it by loosening the two 15-millimeter bolts that secure it to the vehicle. Be sure to save all the original bolts from the bumper and reinforcement bar because some or all (depending on the roll pan you are installing) will be used when installing the aftermarket item.

Before the new roll pan can be secured, use the factory nuts from the old cover to attach four center-angle brackets to the factory cover's slotted mounting holes. These are located on the rear body panels. The brackets should be snug—but not yet. Wait to tighten them because you will need to adjust them up or down to align the roll pan. Use original factory mounting locations and bolts to install the aftermarket reinforcement bar.

From this point on, it's all about reattaching the factory parts to the new roll pan. Attach the factory back-up lights to the threaded inserts on the roll pan using the supplied screws and washers. Plug in the license plate lamp before mounting the roll pan.

Install the factory back-up lamps and license plate light onto the roll pan.

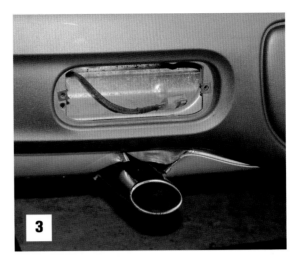

The back-up lamps are removed from the original bumper and will be attached to the new roll pan.

Access the final securing screws from behind the fender well covers. Once these are removed (two on each side), the factory bumper slides to the rear and off.

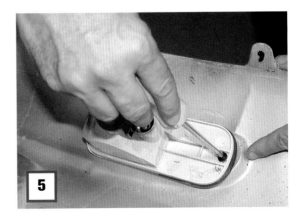

To help prevent scratching the finish of the vehicle or of the freshly painted roll pan, get a couple of other PT Cruiser geeks to hold the new pan in place as you secure it through the wheel wells. When the sides are attached, drill a hole in the center of each angle bracket, using light pressure, and carefully drill through the top edge of the roll pan into the four brackets. Now slide the angle brackets up or down as necessary to align the roll pan with the rear hatch. Use the supplied Phillips head screws to attach the roll pan to the brackets. Do not overtighten the screws because you may bend the roll pan and cause warping or waviness. In many cases, it is necessary to drill holes for screws to attach the fender liner.

For additional security, mount the angle bracket behind the license plate housing using the screws supplied. Hold the bracket flush against center of the license plate housing on the back side of the roll pan and attach it to the floor of vehicle. Drill one hole through the roll pan into the bracket and attach.

It usually takes only a few hours to complete the entire job. From a cosmetic standpoint, it's 120 of the most productive minutes you can invest in your PT.

6: While a fellow PTer lends a hand, reconnect the electrical terminals to the back-up and license plate lights.

7: Slide the new roll pan forward into place.

8: This aftermarket roll pan is molded with factory-matched mounting tracks.

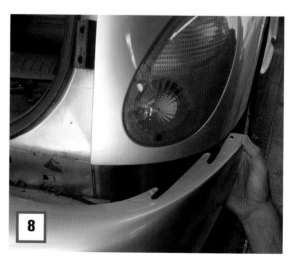

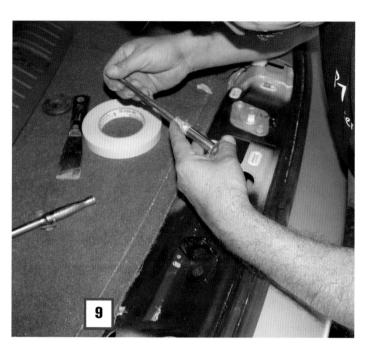

Secure the bumper bolts. A bit of masking tape helps keep the bolts on the socket as the reach back is beyond finger length.

Attach four center angle brackets to the factory cover slotted mounting holes on the rear body panels using factory nuts from the old cover. Note: The brackets should be snug, but not tightened yet, because you may need to adjust them up or down to align the roll pan.

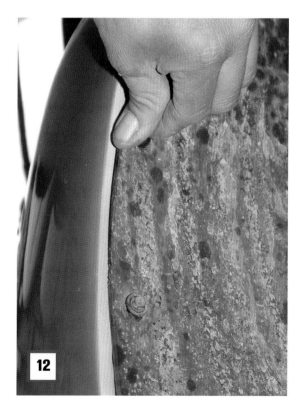

Drill holes for fender liner screws and attach the fender liner.

Reinstall the 7-millimeter screws in the fender well mount. Do not overtighten; this can strip the plastic holes in the roll pan.

PROJECT 18 ★ *Teardrop Taillights*

Time: 10-15 minutes

Tools: Phillips screwdriver, Torx head driver

Talent: ★ (after paint)

Tab: $100

Parts: Teardrop replacements

Tip: Order in matched color

Benefit: Improved appearance

Every so often an accessory is crafted that is so right, it is a sin not to install it. PTeazer's teardrop taillight assemblies are that type of product. These taillights are quick and easy to install, and add so much visual appeal to the rear view of a PT—it is downright amazing. This item was so easy to install that it could be handed over to an eight-year-old and be complete in just a few minutes.

After the assemblies have been painted (in most cases you can order the product pre-painted and ready to install), the entire job requires just a simple Phillips screwdriver or Torx head driver and about five minutes of time for each side. The factory taillights are secured to the PT's exterior by a slip fit and one screw. Simply remove the screw and pull away from the body. The bulb and bulb housing pops out of the original taillight assembly by turning the housing about one-quarter turn counterclockwise. Install the bulb housing in reverse order in the tear drop unit. Attach to the body with the Phillips or Torx head and you're done.

Remove the taillight lenses and lamp assemblies. The teardrop units use the factory lamps, so keep these attached.

Test-fit the taillights to ensure everything is snug and where it should be. The fit and quality of the product used in this install are superb. They feel solid and line up perfectly.

If you order unpainted units, they come pre-primed. Start the prep work by wet sanding with 600-grit paper. The idea here is to give the new paint lots of nooks and crannies to adhere.

3

4

4: Mask the inside portion where the bulbs are housed. The white surface will make the lamps brighter.

5

6

7

5: Wipe down the taillights with a suitable degreaser before painting them. Use smooth motions to minimize the chances of runs or blemishes.

6: Once the paint dries, the factory lamp assemblies are plugged into the taillights and the new units are screwed in place using the reverse of the previously mentioned screwdriver technique.

7: If your taste is more modern than retro street rod, there are modern options such as these full-lamp versions.

PROJECT 19 ★ | *Ram-Air Hood*

Time: 2 hours (after paint)

Tools: Flat screwdriver, standard socket set, needle-nose pliers, large, soft blankets

Talent: ★★

Tab: $800 (not including painting)

Parts: Hood

Tip: Fit first, paint second, install third. Mark hole for alignment.

Benefit: Performance appearance, improved engine cooling, and air intake availability

The purpose of the large, flat factory hood is to protect the engine from the elements and complete the visual aesthetics of the vehicle. The hood does very well on the function side of things, but the fashion side can be improved. An aftermarket hood can also add a bit of performance to the vehicle.

The installation of the lightweight ram-air hood is quite easy, requiring minimal tools and mechanical experience. It will, however, require the aid of a friend, as the full hood can be awkward to handle by yourself.

Start by opening the hood and supporting it with the factory hood prop. Next, use needle-nose pliers to disconnect the window washer nozzles' hoses. It is easiest to first push in on the hoses, which expand the connection point around the nipple. Once the connection point is expanded, give the hose a slight twist and gently pull away from the nipple to remove the hose. Now remove the nozzles from the hood. Do not discard the nozzles; the pair will be relocated later in the installation.

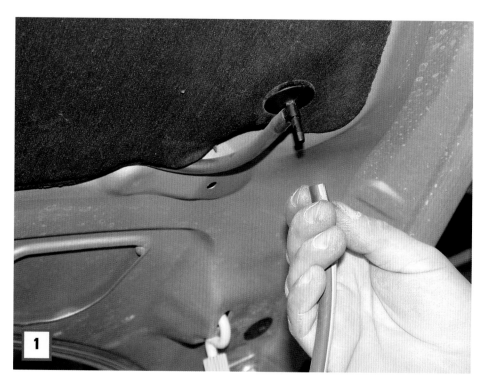

Pop and prop the hood. Remove the windshield washer hoses from the nozzles in the hood.

1

If your model has a ground strap attached to the hood, it is okay to disconnect it at this time.

This is where those large, soft blankets come into play. Spread out the blankets on a flat work surface. Be sure the surface is clean and free of any tools, debris, or other items that could damage the painted surface of the factory and/or aftermarket hood. With help from a friend, loosen the four 13-millimeter nuts that connect the hood and the hinges. Save the hardware for future use. Remove the factory hood and lay it upside down on the blankets. Position the aftermarket hood next to the factory hood, also in the upside-down position.

Before installing the ram-air hood, you will need to relocate the windshield wiper nozzles. Included with this ram-air hood is an easy-to-use template that enables you to relocate the nozzles in the ideal position. Begin by removing the clips that attach the factory heat insulation to the underside of the hood. This allows you access to the factory nozzles, housings, and hoses. To remove the insulation, pop off the attachment clips (each looks like a plastic version of a nuclear warning symbol). The nozzles and hoses are hidden by the insulation. Unclip the hoses and nozzles; clean and treat each in preparation for relocation.

Moving back to the PT, align the template and mark where the new nozzle holes will be drilled. Remove the windshield wiper arms (13 millimeters) and protective cowl shrouding. Working on a flat work surface, drill two small holes with a 1/8-inch bit, duplicating the shape of the holes on the original hood. Make sure you do not make the holes too large. The first hole should be located almost in

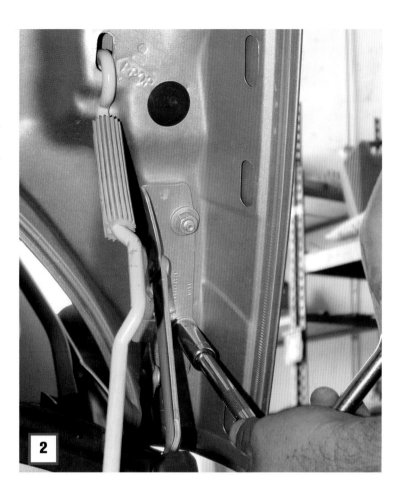

Remove the four bolts (two per side) that hold the hood to the hinges.

The hood is large and can be awkward to handle for one person; use the buddy system as you remove it.

the center of the windshield and angled slightly to the passenger side, approximately 1/2 inch from the edge of the cowl panel and next to the wiper mount. The second hole should be placed 13 inches from the first, pointing at the driver, and 1/2 inch from the edge of the cowling. Plug the existing hoses into the nozzles and reinstall the cowl panel and wipers. Once this is completed, reattach the cowl shroud and wipers.

Use the buddy system to lift the ram-air hood onto the factory hinges. Carefully install the mounting bolts—do not completely tighten the bolts until both sides are equally installed. Once all four bolts are lightly tightened, secure each of them but do not overtighten. The final step is to remove the original hood latch (10 millimeters) from the factory hood and mount it in the exact same position on the new ram-air hood. This is a simple two-bolt procedure. Carefully close the hood until you are confident of the alignment and fit. Because the ram-air hood used in this install was a very well engineered item, the fit and finish was nearly perfect the first time. Adjustments should not be necessary.

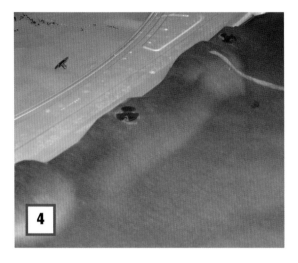

4

With the hood placed upside down on a protective and flat work surface, remove the clips that hold on the factory insulation.

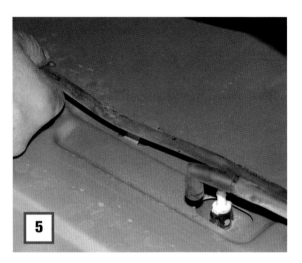

5

Lift off the insulation to gain access to the windshield washer hoses and nozzles. Unclip and remove the hoses, nozzles, and housings.

Remove the windshield wiper arms from the vehicle.

6

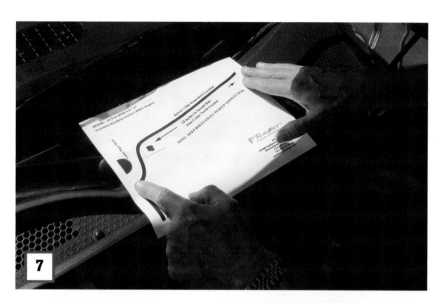

Use the washer-nozzle hole template to mark the new location of the windshield wiper nozzles.

7

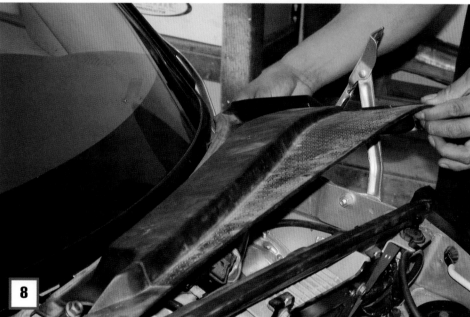

Next, remove the cowl shrouding by way of the 10 Phillips screws.

9: Drill the holes for the nozzles.

10: Attach the nozzles and nozzle housings to the shrouding.

8

9

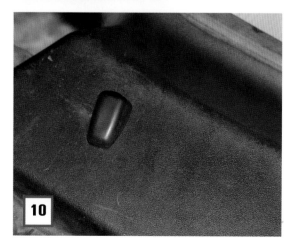

10

79

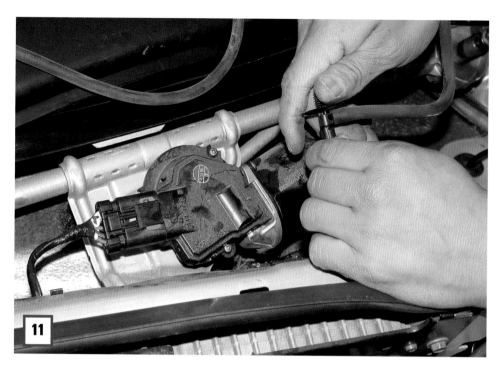

Attach the washer hoses to the washer fluid pump. Before securing the shroud pieces, attach the washer hoses to the nozzles.

Attach the new ram-air hood to the hood hinges.

Attach the factory hood latch to the correct position on the underside of the hood.

Close the hood and enjoy!

PROJECT 20 ★ *Shorty Antenna*

Time: 5 minutes

Tools: Pliers, 3/8-inch wrench

Talent: ★

Tab: $30

Parts: Shorty antenna

Tip: Use tape and a plastic hosing to protect the finish

Benefit: Better appearance

There are a few very fine quick fixes for the low-budget modification blues. One of these fixes is the shorty antenna. This item installs in a few minutes and requires no special tools or talents. Its main benefit is that it gets rid of the factory fishing pole antenna Chrysler screwed on right before the vehicle left its Mexico assembly plant.

Don't be mistaken or misled—the shorty antenna offers no additional radio signal reception, no added performance benefit, and no functional value. This modification is strictly cosmetic.

Installing this item is simple enough for anyone to do it. All that is required (barely) is a pair of pliers. For the overcautious, a few strips of masking tape can be placed on the painted surface around the antenna's body mounting point. This will help prevent paint damage if your grip slips and the pliers go flying out of control.

Remove the factory buggy-whip antenna by gripping the base of the unit with a 3/8-inch wrench. Turn counterclockwise about 1/4 turn. Remove the wrench and turn by hand until the antenna is free.

Before installing the shorty antenna, cut a piece of rubber hose about 1 inch in length. Fit the new antenna in place and hand-tighten. Fit the hose over the base of the shorty antenna. Using a pair of pliers, grasp the base of the protected antenna and tighten. Be sure not to get too aggressive; the pliers may scrape the body.

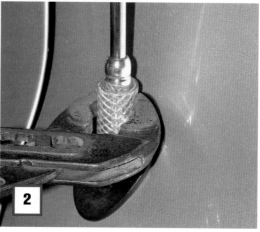

1: Remove the factory antenna and inset the new antenna onto the same factory mounting position.

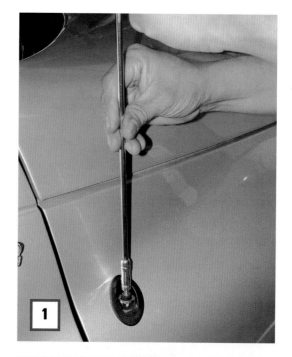

2: Slide the rubber hose over the antenna and onto its base. Tighten with pliers, using the rubber hose to protect the antenna's finish.

PROJECT 21 ★ *Fuel Filler Door*

Time: 10-15 minutes

Tools: Allen wrench, socket driver, Torx fitting

Talent: ★

Tab: $75

Parts: Performance-style fuel filler door

Benefit: Better appearance

Over the past few years, one of the biggest rages in automotive styling has been the performance fuel filler door. In reality, these items are no more than fancy gas hole covers. Despite the fact that a performance fuel filler door provides no additional performance (not even when you're filling up), nor any beneficial function, they are a staple item in Customizing 101. If a performance fuel door cover does nothing else, it does provide a point of difference between nonmodified and slightly modified PTs.

Performing a gas door cover swap takes only a few minutes and requires no special mechanical skills. It does, however, require a Torx fitting wrench.

To begin, pop the factory gas door open. There are two Torx nuts and a leash that secures the gas cap to the door. Disconnect the leash from the gas door by simply popping it out of its place on the filler cap.

Firmly grasp the gas door and remove the two Torx nuts. This will free the door from the body. Slip mounting clips over the existing holes vacated by the Torx nuts. Place the performance fuel filler door in place. Its exterior is rimmed with Allen head fasteners. Only two are used to secure the door to the body. Back up the two mounting fasteners with supplied washers and nuts. Tighten the Allen heads, and you're ready to add fuel.

Pop open the door. The only special tool needed is a Torx head driver to remove the two screws that secure the door to the body.

83

Undo the door leash from the door.

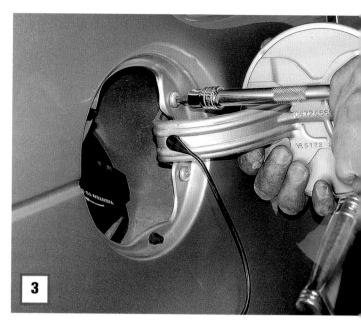

Remove the two Torx head screws from the body.

The gas hole is now ready to be customized.

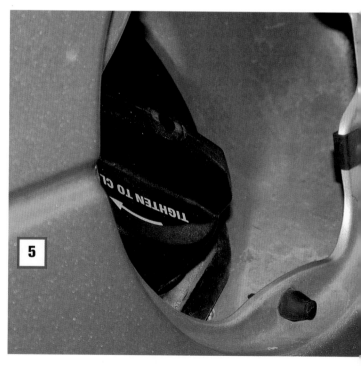

Slip the Allen bolt clips over the securing holes.

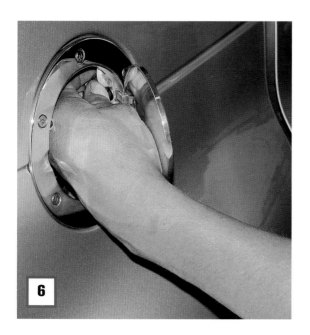

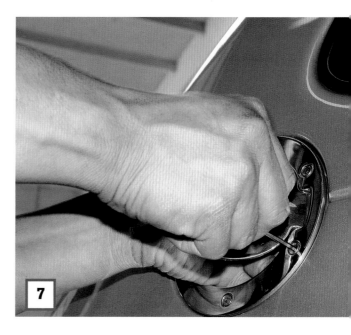

Place the trick fuel filler door in place and back up the Allen head fasteners with supplied hardware.

Tighten down the bolts.

Close the door and head for the nearest gas station.

PROJECT 22 ★ *The Details of Shine*

Time: 1-5 hours

Tools: Elbow grease

Talent: ★

Tab: $10-$300

Parts: Wash bucket, water, hose, wax and polishes, clean cloths, drying chamois, shade

Tip: Never wash and polish in direct sun

Benefit: Better appearance, longer life for paint, rubber, metal, leather, and vinyl

Remember the way that your PT looked when you first drove it off the dealer's lot? Over time, various environmental factors cause paint to fade and no longer look like new. Whether your Cruiser still looks good, or it is starting to show signs of aging or road wear, caring for the paint is a vital step in preserving a premium appearance. There are multiple chemicals and compounds available that, when used properly, can make the paint look outstanding.

Choosing the right product to do the job may be the most difficult part. There are several products out there, ranging from waxes that are applied with an aerosol can to products that require professional knowledge and tools to use properly. Low-end synthetic and "quick" waxes will never provide the same level of shine that can be achieved by using professional products.

Many companies claim their products provide a professional-looking finish without the amount of work and time that professional products require. With a bit of research and careful selection, modern technology has made it possible to purchase products that deliver professional results. The key is selecting a line or combination of detailing products that work together for washing, preparing, polishing, and waxing. This may include sponges, cloths, and a chamois.

Properly detailing your PT is more involved than "wax on, wax off." Wait for a day when the temperature is between 65 and 85 degrees. Avoid detailing the car in direct sunlight. For optimum results, the surface of the paint should remain cool. This can be done by using a garage, covering, or choosing a day with a lot of cloud cover. Obviously, these ideal conditions are not possible in the dead of winter or in the middle of summer, but use them as a guide.

Begin by washing the car thoroughly with soap specifically designed for automobiles. Car wash soaps are specially formulated to gently cleanse automobile paint, reducing the risk of damage. Completely rinse the car and begin to scrub away dirt and grime with

1

On factory chrome-plated wheels, a good window cleaner works very well. Combined with a rubber cleaner and a tire cleaning brush, spiffing up the tires and wheels can be quick and easy. Start by applying your tire and wheel cleaners.

Using a tire brush will remove road grime baked on by the heat of the tires. It's amazing how grimy the rubber gets, even in a short period of time.

either a soft brush or a wash mitt. A sponge is not recommended as it can store dirt and debris in its cavities. Using too much force could scratch the paint. Rub lightly and repeatedly, allowing the soap and bubbles to lift the dirt away from the car. If the washing is taking place on a hot day, wash one section at a time and rinse the area before the soap dries on the painted surface.

Don't forget to wash the wheels. Tar, brake dust, and other elements can cause wheels to look dull. To

break up contaminants, use a wheel cleaner that is safe to use on all wheels. Let it soak for a few minutes, then scrub it with a sponge and rinse. Drying the wheels immediately after washing them will help to prevent water spots. Due to the potential of picking up leftover brake dust, don't use the chamois

Use a generous amount of water to rinse the tires and wheels clean.

If you're feeling especially ambitious, there is a quick and easy way to make your engine compartment clean enough to eat off of it. Start with a cool engine. As a precaution, drape a few clean towels over the fenders. This will keep unwanted chemicals from landing on the paint surface.

Spray rubber cleaner on the entire engine compartment.

6

for drying your wheels. Use a disposable cloth or a clean rag.

A natural or synthetic chamois should be used to dry the vehicle. Both a synthetic chamois and a natural chamois will not leave streaks, lint, or scratches on the paint surface like a conventional cotton or fiber towel. The additional advantage of a synthetic chamois is that it can absorb a higher degree of water, and it can be stored wet because it is treated to prevent mold. This leaves it soft and pliable for the next use.

If synthetic wax or paint sealer was used on the car recently (a common up-charge from the dealer), remove it using a wax stripper before continuing. This will provide the best results because synthetic waxes and natural carnauba waxes do not mix. When used together, they can leave a hazy finish.

Run your hand over the paint surface to check for smoothness. Environmental fallout, sap, and other elements adhere to the paint and cause it to feel rough. Normal washing will not remove these contaminants. For best results, these contaminants should be removed before polishing or waxing. By using a clay bar and a paint surface lubricant, such as Griot's Speed Shine, these contaminants can be easily removed. Take a piece of clay about the size of a silver dollar and form it into a flat rectangle or circle. Next, spray some Speed Shine on the paint surface. The Speed Shine will act as a lubricant while the clay is rubbed over the surface, picking up tiny particles

along the way. Once a small area has been completed, wipe the area dry with a soft, clean towel. Now the area should feel very smooth.

Once the clay bar has been used on the entire vehicle, the next step is to polish the paint. The goal here is to remove oxidization and small scratches in order to reveal the natural color and shine of the paint. Polishing can be done either by hand or machine; however, it is important to get the proper

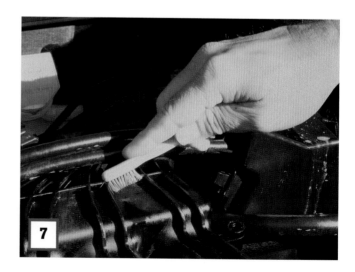

7

While the rubber cleaner is eating away the grime, use a toothbrush to clean hard-to-reach areas.

Rinse the entire engine bay with water. To help the drying process, close the hood and run the engine for several minutes.

polish for the job. Use a hand polish and apply it with a polishing pad. Work the product into the paint one section at a time in a small, circular motion. Buff each section with a clean, dry polishing towel.

After the paint has been completely cleaned and polished, it is time to protect the finish with a good coat of wax. For the deepest shine and best results, use a carnauba wax. As with the polish, the wax can also be applied by hand or by machine. It is recommended that the wax be applied with a soft sponge. Apply the wax in a small, circular motion. Very little wax is needed and it should be easy to wipe off when dry. Once a section has dried, buff the wax away with a soft cloth. A section may need to be buffed a few times in order to remove all of the wax.

Now that the paint is protected, it's time to move to the tires and wheels. Use a rag or towel to apply vinyl dressing to the tires as well. Finally, go over the windows with high-quality window cleaner and disposable towels.

It is truly amazing what a little work and high-quality products will do for aged paint. The process can take about four hours to complete, but it will provide extremely impressive results. With a little elbow grease, your PT will come out brilliant. The shine will be so deep that it looks as if the vehicle was just dipped in paint and is still in the process of drying. These products yield very impressive results, and they can be used by anyone in their own garage without special tools or know-how.

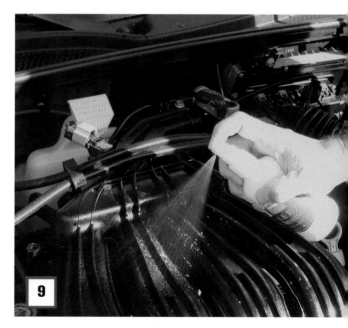

After the engine is dry, spray the entire bay with a rubber treatment.

Now close the hood and wash the exterior of the PT. It is important to use the right products. Never use a household soap, such as laundry or dish soap, to wash your PT. Use quality car wash soap. Beginning at the top of the vehicle and working down, rinse the car with water.

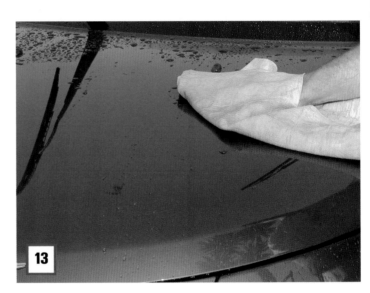

11, 12, 13: Scrub the car using a soft brush (use only a brush designed for cleaning cars) or a wool mitt. Clean all areas including emblems and lights. Be sure to rinse the soap from the car before it begins to dry. Then dry the car with a microfiber towel (as shown here), a chamois, or a soft, cotton towel.

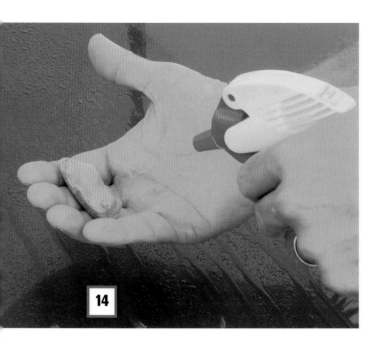

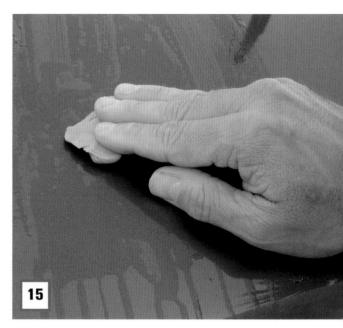

14, 15, 16: A clay bar is a good way to remove surface contaminants. Shape the bar into a flat rectangle. Spray the surface of the car with a quick detailing spray and then rub the bar over the surface. Once an area has been completed, wipe it dry with a soft towel.

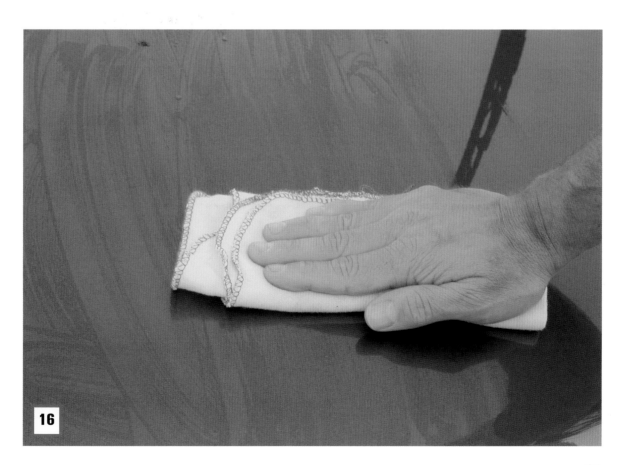

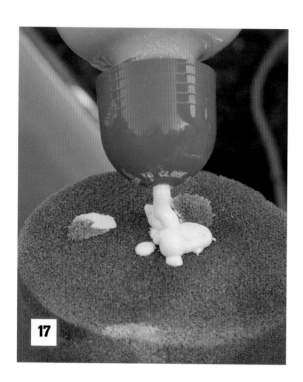

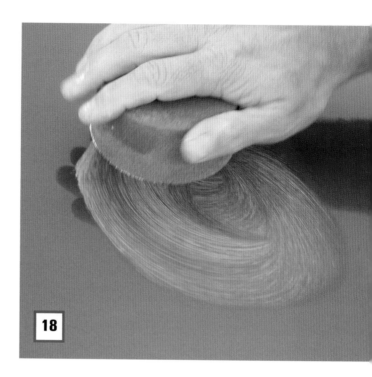

17, 18, 19: A good polish will remove oxidization and small scratches. Apply the polish with an applicator pad and work it into the paint with a small circular motion. Some detailers recommend using a straight front-to-back motion to minimize the possibility of introducing swirl marks. Buff the polish with a soft towel until it has all been removed.

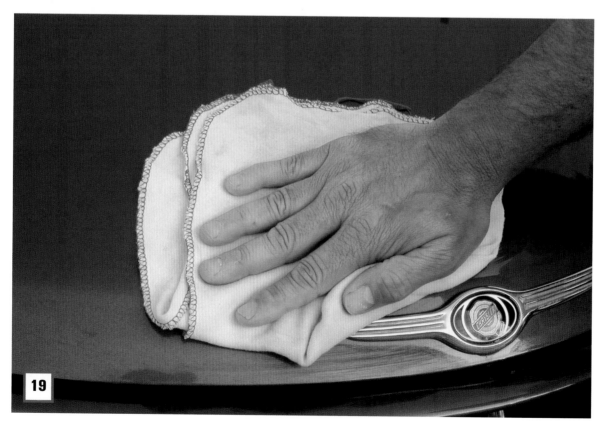

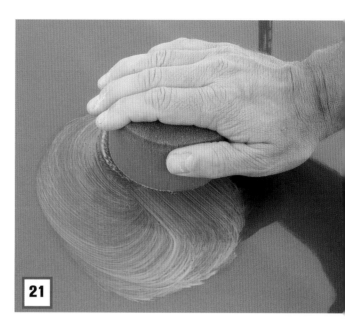

20, 21: Use quality carnauba wax and apply it with a soft sponge. A light coat is all that is needed. Once the wax has dried, wipe it off with a soft towel.

Now pop the hood and check out the engine compartment. With the vinyl and rubber treatment dry, the engine bay looks like you spent all day with your head under the hood.

22, 23: Finish the job with a window cleaner and a lint-free towel.

PROJECT 23 ★ *Painting on Personality*

Time: 10-36 hours

Tools: Tape, masking paper, air compressor, paint gun, art blades, striping brush

Talent: ★★★★

Tab: $250 – $3,000

Parts: Automotive paint (two-step)

Tip: If you're not an expert . . . hire one

Benefit: Improved appearance, personal touch

You can mark the passing of time by the emerging and passing of custom paint schemes. In the early 1950s, the interest in hot rodding created an opportunity for self-expression in the form of paint treatments that were anything but conservative. The era brought to light the talents of Von Dutch, Watson, Roth, Windfield, and Barris.

By the 1960s, custom paint had become an everyday sight at cruise spots, races, and drive-in burger joints—especially in the car-crazy culture of California.

With the advent of the van craze in the 1970s, murals were used to fill the massive metal canvases of domestic panels. The 1980s saw the resurfacing of multi-layer panel designs. The mini-truck movement of the 1990s brought about full-blown graphics, combining a variety of styles and treatments.

Today, the PT Cruiser is the new canvas of choice in the customizing world. It is not unusual to see a wide range of paint treatments when attending a show or event. Flames, murals, wide striping, panels, pearls, ghost flames, foils, gold and/or silver leaf; the possibilities are endless and bordered only by the imagination and ability of the painter.

Paint enhancements are a very personal matter. What makes the PT Cruiser a unique canvas is that all styles and variations of paint seem to work equally well on the vehicle's distinctive lines. The flowing fender lines and flat hood give flames movement, similar to the fenders of a street rod. The ideally proportioned side doors allow multi-layer panel graphics or scallops to be laid out in an infinite number of shapes and color combinations. The flat rear hatch is perfect for murals or accent pin striping.

Of all custom paint treatments, flames have stood the test of time. Flames, in one form or another, have been a popular style for more than 50 years. From massive fat licks to elongated fingers, to candy colors and pearlescent ghosted images, flames have been the cornerstone of the custom paint world. The look has become so popular that Chrysler offers a factory-flame job, although it is achieved with vinyl.

As popular as any factory paint scheme may become, nothing can match the individual touch of custom paint applied by a professional custom automotive painter.

Customized paint is a very involved process. From preparation to layout, cutting, buffing, and

Begin the paint process by scuffing the clear coat from the body panels to be painted.

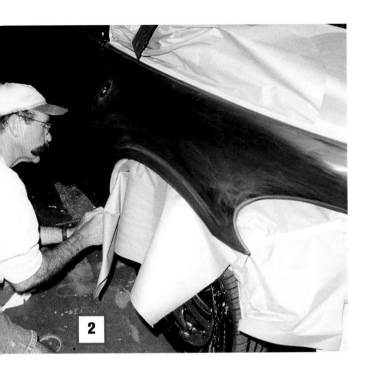

2

Use extensive masking to protect the remainder of the vehicle from overspray.

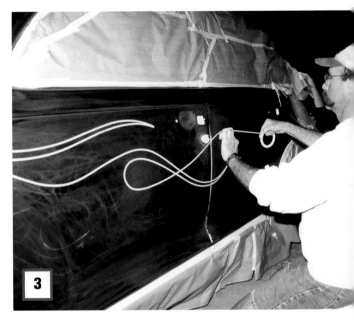

3

Lay out the flames by using thin masking tape.

4

Cut crossover areas to allow for even flow of color.

finishing, a good custom painter will require a week to do most styles right. Before making a decision about which painter to use, interview many. Ask to see their work or take a few hours to watch them perform. Once the paint is on, you want to be completely happy with the results.

If you're going to attempt to do the job yourself, get to know your local paint and body shop supply house. There are many products that can help make the job easier—such as full adhesive masking paper, chalk socks, perforation tools, and special brushes.

Of all possible styles, flames are by far the most popular custom-paint choice of PT enthusiasts. For pre-2003 models, you may want to opt for the smooth front bumper look by sanding off the bumper's texture. A better option may be to select an aftermarket item (see Project 16) or a 2003 front bumper assembly from your local Chrysler dealer.

Nearly all custom paint treatments require the same basic procedures: strip, prep, paint, finish. Begin by laying out the basic design. Scuff the clear coat using a special 3M Scotchbrite pad. Mask the areas to be unpainted with automotive-grade masking tape and masking paper.

When painting flames, lay out the licks using 1/8-inch or 1/4-inch masking tape. The thinner the

tape, the easier it will be to form the flame's curves. The crossover licks give the flames depth and dimension. The crossovers are cut to allow for even color flow. Pinstriping will finish the over-under effect.

Once the flames have been fully laid out, apply firm finger pressure to all the taped areas. Remember to mask off the areas that will remain unpainted. This process will take a while, but is well worth the effort because it will help prevent overspray from falling on the body.

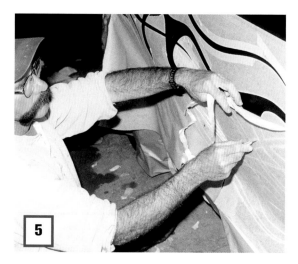

Cover exposed body panels by using special masking paper. Carefully cut the flame design out of the paper. Use just the right amount of pressure. Too little, and the paper will not cut with a crisp edge. Too much pressure, and damage can be done to the finish.

Once the masking process is complete, wipe down the exposed areas with a light degreaser or thinner. This step will remove dust and other airborne objects from the surface so that it is ready to be painted. Mix the colors and begin spraying. You will likely be using a two-step paint process of a D-Base and clear coat. D-Base paints dry flat with little or no sheen. The clear coat that comes later adds the deep gloss. When shooting flames (or any design that has crossover areas), pay close attention to the crossovers to ensure consistent color flow. This will be important when adding the pinstriping.

D-Base paint dries quickly, reducing the time it takes between colors. When you're satisfied with the colors and coverage, shut down the gun and let the entire job sit for a minimum of 12 hours. Apply the clear coat and let it dry for another 12 hours.

The next steps are wet-sanding and buffing the painted areas. Follow this up by pinstriping the flames.

Before spraying the color, brew a precise mixture of paint, thinner, and curing agent. This mix will help the paint to spray evenly and dry in preparation for the next round of colors.

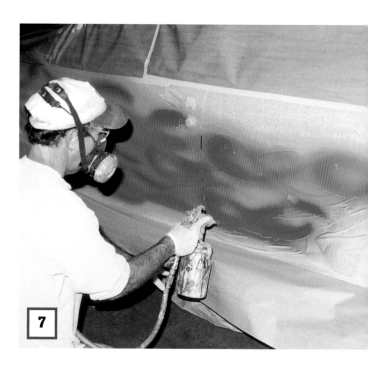

After completing the final masking and the paint is mixed, add color to the pattern. In this case, the yellow was laid down first, followed by red.

96

Pay careful attention to the crossover areas. Here, red was shot over yellow, then yellow was reloaded to highlight back over the red.

8

With the paint applied, the next steps are to clear coat, wet-sand, buff, and pinstripe.

9

The completed job took about three days (allowing time for all coats to dry before cutting, buffing, and striping. A flame job turned this black Cruiser into a true street custom and helped to highlight the other modifications to the vehicle.

10

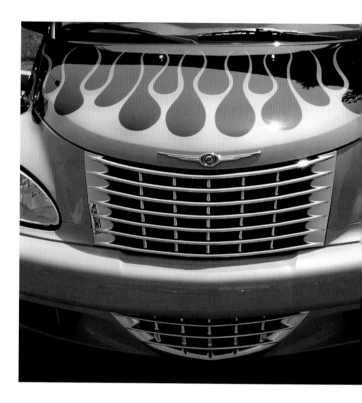

(Clockwise) Flames and PTs were made for each other. There are several styles. The blue flames feature long licks. The more traditional hot rod flames engulf the hood and front grille, and then work back. New-age flames highlight specific areas. Vintage-style hot rod flames work PT fenders like a dream. The latest trend is art flames that project a feeling of movement.

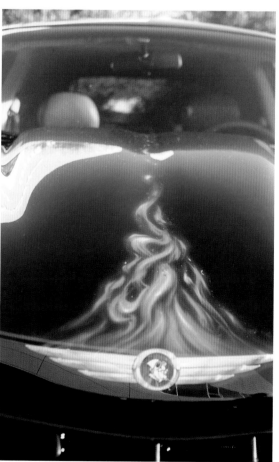

Murals were once the art form of choice for vans and low riders. Now PT Cruisers are the muralist's automotive canvas of choice. From a simple theme to complex and extensive multi-image masterpieces, the panels of the PT are perfect for all styles.

Above left, above, left: Graphics have come in and out of style—from customs of the 1950s and 1960s to vans of the 1970s and mini-trucks of the late 1980s and early 1990s. Different graphic styles play well on the PT's body lines.

PROJECT 24 ★ *Billet Door Sill Covers*

Time: 1 hour

Tools: Power drill, 1/8-inch drill bit, flathead and Phillips head screwdrivers, sheet of thin cardboard

Talent: ★★

Tab: $120

Parts: New door sill covers

Tip: Measure twice – drill once

Benefit: Improved appearance

The interior of the PT Cruiser is a very well designed and ergonomically pleasing package. The seats are at the ideal height and angle for about 95 percent of drivers and the shoulder, hip, and legroom can accommodate a wide variety of passengers. The steering wheel mounting provides ample visibility to the gauge cluster and the controls are placed well for easy adjustment. So, with all this going for it, what do you replace or improve on your PT?

For those without the factory leather package (Limited Edition, GT, and Dream Cruiser) there is the option of swapping out the cloth seat (fore and aft) for leather. This is a matter of locating the front and rear seating from a salvage yard and simply turning a few wrenches.

Aside from that, to find a quick and easy upgrade, just open all four doors and gaze at the area where the painted body ends and the interior trim begins. This is called a door sill. Plastic sill covers are installed at the factory. These black items are very functional and act as a nonslip/skid aid when entering or exiting the vehicle. They do their job, but as far as appearance, plastic door sill covers are just one step above Coke bottle glasses on a librarian.

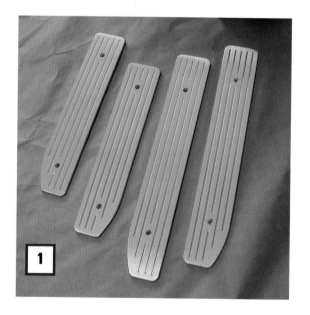

1

These billet aluminum sill plate covers provide fashion and function. Although not intended to be slip-proof or resistant, they do add beauty over the factory plastic plates. Before starting, check-fit all four plates as there are specific left- and right-side plates for both the front and rear door sills.

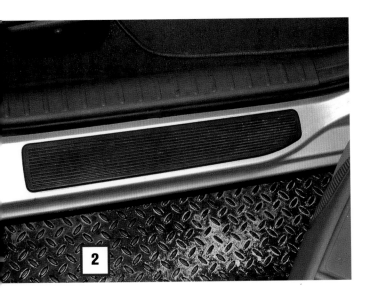

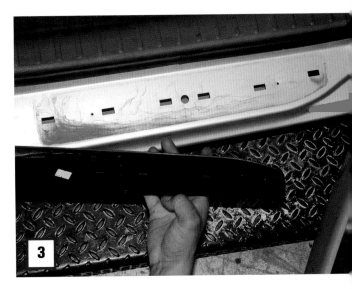

The first order of business is to pry off the plastic covers.

Use a flathead screwdriver to remove the factory covers. It's a good idea to clean the painted surface after removing the covers because dirt and debris gather under the covers.

Also, Chrysler only installed (on most models) front door plastic door sill covers—there are none on the rear doors.

A quick fix for the plastic sill cover blues is polished door steps. Generally made from billet aluminum, these items install with minimal effort

and return a bright trim appearance when the door(s) are opened.

Allow about 60 minutes to complete the install. First you will need to remove the factory plastic door

Position the billet cover on the sill, mark the hole position, and drill. Secure the plate with one of the self-tapping screws.

sill covers (or, as Chrysler calls them, "scuff plates"). To help protect the painted surface from potential damage, use a thin sheet of cardboard, such as the backing of a writing tablet, and slip it under the existing rubber cover. Using a flathead screwdriver, slide the blade of it under the sill cover and gently pry the cover up. Over time, dirt finds its way under the sill covers. Clean the door sill and jamb area before installing the new covers.

Start with the front by test-fitting the new covers. There is a specific left- and right-side plate. Beginning on the left side of the vehicle, position the new billet cover evenly in place and mark the screw hole positions with a marker or scribe tool. Lift the cover off and drill a 1/8-inch hole in the front position. Attach the plate using one of the included self-tapping screws. With the plate in the correct position, apply firm pressure as you drill a 1/8-inch hole for the rear screw. Finish mounting the plate by securing the rear self-tapping screw. Repeat the process for the right side front sill plate.

The rear passenger doors of the PT are void of the factory plastic scuff plates. Therefore, beginning on the right side, position the billet plate evenly on the door sill and mark the screw hole positions. Lift the plate off and drill a 1/8-inch hole in the front marked position. Attach the plate using a self-tapping screw. With the plate in position, apply firm pressure as you drill a 1/8-inch hole for the rear screw. Finish mounting the plate by securing the rear self-tapping screw. Repeat the process for the left-side rear sill plate.

Because these are scuff plates, originally designed to protect the painted finish of the door jam, they will take some abuse, causing them to scratch. Use a billet aluminum polish to buff out fine blemishes.

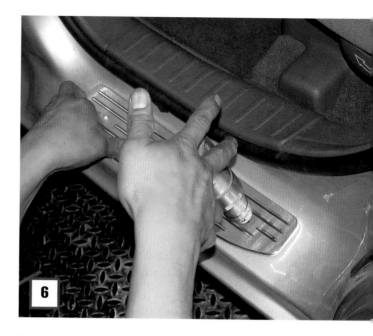

6

Repeat the process on the rear sill. The one exception to the procedure is that the rear sills do not have the factory plastic covers to remove.

7

Secure the rear sill plate covers.

5

Once the front of the sill plate is secure, drill the rear screw hole and secure.

PROJECT 25 ★ *Pedals and Knobs*

Time: 1 hour

Tools: Power drill, 1/8-inch drill bit, flathead and Phillips head screwdrivers

Talent: ★ ★

Tab: $125

Parts: Foot pedals and door lock knobs

Tip: Measure twice – drill once

Benefit: Improved appearance

Much like the factory plastic scuff plates, the PT's pedal covers are designed to be strictly functional. To that end, as an enthusiast, here is an opportunity to take the step Chrysler either wouldn't or couldn't add.

Billet aluminum pedal covers provide an easy cosmetic upgrade, although they offer no additional function. On the other hand, these covers do not impede or hamper the operation of the brake or accelerator pedals. At the time of publishing, pedal kits were available for automatic transmission models only.

It is necessary to remove the factory pedal pads. The pedal pad can be lifted from the metal pedal by leveraging the upper left corner of the pads. In some cases, it is easier to use a flathead screwdriver blade to get the process started. Once the inner lip of the pad is over the pedal, the removal becomes quite easy. Because the new billet covers are slightly larger then the factory rubber covers, it is easier to remove both the factory accelerator and brake pedal covers before installing the billet covers.

Once the pedals are free of the factory covers, wipe down the pedals with a cleaning solvent. This step simply removes any dust or debris that may have adhered to the pedal's surface.

Begin the installation with the accelerator pedal. Test-fit the billet cover. Mark the screw holes with a marker or scribe tool. Remove the cover and drill through the pedal. Insert and tighten one of the self-tapping screws included in the package. Drill the lower hole and secure the lower screw.

The brake pedal requires you to check the measurements prior to drilling. Place the billet cover over the brake pedal. Mark the holes with a marker or scribe tool. Remove the cover and check the location of the marks. The outer apex of each mark should be at minimum 1/8 inch from the outer edges of the pedal face. If this is true, check-fit the brake pedal cover a second time. Using the cover as a guide, hold it firmly on the pedal face and drill a 1/8-inch hole in the indicated spot. Secure the cover with a screw and drill the second hole. Finish the install by securing the second screw.

You will find that the pedals feel slightly more rigid. For performance purposes, you may find the transmission of feedback to the ball of your foot from the aluminum pedals is less intense. The grip may

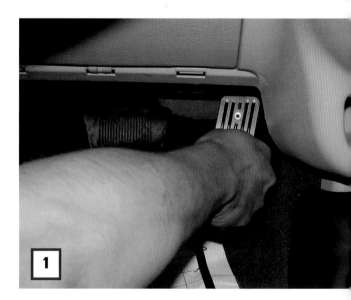

Remove the factory rubber accelerator pedal cover. Fit the billet cover over the pedal face and mark the hole locations.

also be compromised when driving with wet or dampened shoes. However, no one can deny that the billet covers look far better than the rubber, factory-issue covers.

A set of spun aluminun door lock knob covers will complement the pedal covers nicely. To install, simply turn the factory knobs counterclockwise and toss them into the trash. Replace the knobs with the aluminum pieces by twisting them clockwise until tight.

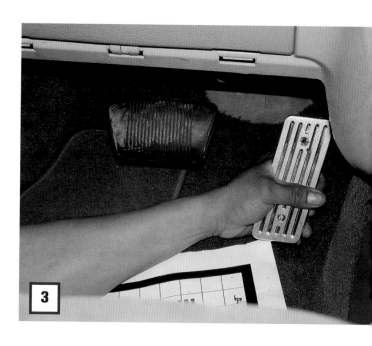

Drill 1/8-inch holes in the pedal face. You can use the billet cover as a guide. Secure the pedal with the screws included in the package.

Remove the factory brake pedal cover.

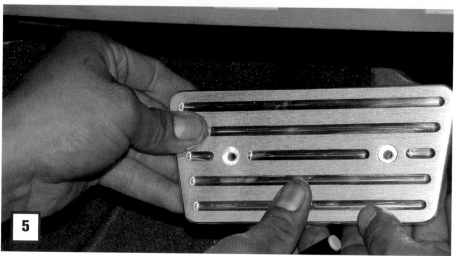

Fit the billet cover over the pedal face and mark the position for the mounting holes.

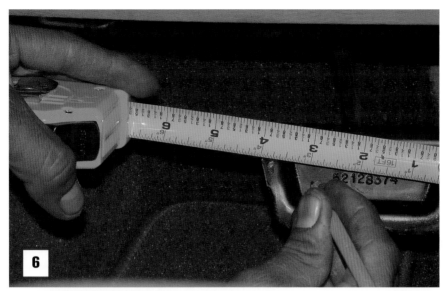

Before drilling the mounting holes, measure to ensure that there is a minimum of 1/8 inch of space between the outer apex of the mounting hole and the edge of the pedal face. Then drill the mounting holes. You can use the cover as a guide.

Mount the pedal cover and secure with the enclosed screws.

Job complete. Due to the metal shavings created by drilling the mounting holes, you should vacuum the driver's side foot area.

PROJECT 26 ★ *Performance Shifter*

Time: 2 hours

Tools: Power drill, flathead and Phillips head screwdrivers

Talent: ★★

Tab: $180 – $225

Parts: Shifter kit

Tip: Prepare a work surface outside the interior

Benefit: Quicker, shorter shifts, more comfortable shifting position

On an annual basis, Chrysler produces about 25 percent of its PT Cruisers with a five-speed manual transmission. For these owners, the thrill of being more closely connected to the driving of their PT is important. The need to feel and control the power band through optimum shifting can make the driver feel like an intricate working part of the vehicle.

No one in his or her right mind will confuse a PT with a sports car, but that doesn't mean it can't feel like one. The factory-installed shifter is by no means a bad unit. In fact, it negotiates shifts quite adequately. However, for those who want to reduce shift throws by 30 percent, slamming the gears quicker with greater precision, a short shift kit is the way to go.

The conversion from factory to quick shifter is not that complex and it can be mastered with just a small amount of mechanical knowledge and a bit of confidence. Step one is to remove the shift knob by applying moderate force as you pull up on the knob. If the shift knob on your PT requires more effort, place an open-end wrench under the knob and gently tap up the underside of the wrench with a hammer or mallet until the knob pops loose.

Next, remove the center console by removing the four mounting screws. Two are located in the cup holder area closest to the dash. The other two are on each side of the rear cup holder. Lift the console up and over the shifter. This may require a small amount of maneuvering.

Once the console is out of the way, locate the clips that hold the shift cable to the shifter frame. These clips are located on the front right corner of the frame. The cables are connected to the shifter lever with a rubber compression fitting. Using a flathead screwdriver, pry the clips off. Remove the four nuts that hold the shifter in place. The shifter can now be lifted from the shifter frame.

Disassemble the factory shifter on a table or workbench. Pay close attention to the return spring and actuator that must be installed into the exact same position when the short shifter is assembled. Load up the new shifter bushing with a generous amount of the grease that is included with the shifter kit. At this point, attach the factory actuator and spring to the new short shifter lever.

Back inside the vehicle, install the longer studs in the bottom of the shifter mechanism. Install the

1

Remove the factory shift knob by applying pressure skyward. An open-end wrench and a mallet or hammer can be used as a gentle persuader, if necessary.

shifter bracket with new bushings. These bushings contribute to the reduction in the overall height of the shifter. Some short shifter kits use a sleeved bolt to act as the cable lever actuator. This is easily threaded into the lever and is used to attach the cable to the shifter.

From this point, the end is near. Install the shifter unit back into the vehicle. Slip the cables over their respective bolts and insert the factory compression washers. Set the lever stops and reinstall the console. Attach the enclosed knob (or any shift knob that fits your hand or fancy) and the installation is complete.

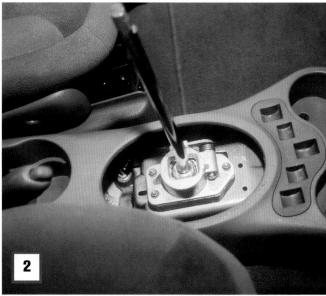

2: Using a flathead screwdriver, pry the shifter boot from the console.

3: Remove the four screws that hold the console in place.

Remove the console to expose the shifter and shifter frame.

Locate the crossover cable (driver's side of the shifter).

Remove the four nuts of the shifter housing.

Using a flathead screwdriver, pop off the clips that hold the cable to the shifter arm.

Disassemble the factory shifter to extract the actuator and spring from the factory shifter. These items will be used again as part of the short shifter kit.

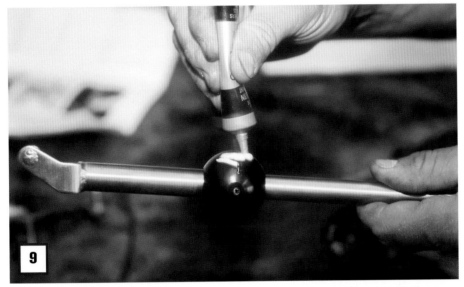

Apply grease (included in the kit) to the bushing.

Slide the new shifter mount onto the shaft. Install the shifter by securing to the shifter frame and attaching the cable with the factory compression fittings. Install the console and boot, then attach the shift knob.

Resources

The Drop Zone
1208 West 9th Street
Upland, California 91786
909-608-0015
info@dzmotorspotts.com
(air ride suspension)

Eibach Springs
17817 Gillette Avenue
Irvine, California 92614
949-752-6780
(performance springs, anti-roll bars)

K&N Filters
1455 Citrus Avenue
Riverside, CA 92507
800-858-3333
www.knfilters.com
(performance air filters)

IGNITION SOLUTIONS
7920 Silverton Avenue Ste E
San Diego, CA 92126
858-586-0080
www.ignitionsolutions.com

Jackson Racing
440 Rutherford Street
Goleta, California 93117
714-891-1113
www.supercharger.com
(superchargers)

Hahn Racecraft
1981 D. Wiesbrock Drive
Oswego, IL 60543
630-801-1417
www.hahnracecraft.com
(turbochargers)

PTeazer
14600 Goldenwest Street Ste A105
Westminster, CA 92683
714-903-9000
www.pteazer.com
(grilles and fascias, teardrop taillights,
ram-air hoods)

PTcruisn
17736 Slover Avenue
Bloomington, CA 92316
800-251-2448
(rear roll pans)

Kustom Auto Graphics
1277 North Cuyamaca Avenue
El Cajon, California 92020
619-698-1634
(teardrop taillights)

Index

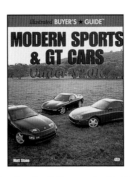

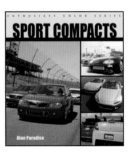